WELL-PRESERVED

ALSO BY EUGENIA BONE

At Mesa's Edge

Italian Family Dining

WELL-PRESERVED

recipes and techniques for putting up
small batches of seasonal foods

EUGENIA BONE

photographs by
Megan Schlow and Andrew Brucker

Clarkson Potter/Publishers
New York

Published in the United States by Clarkson Potter/
Publishers, an imprint of the Crown Publishing Group,
a division of Random House, Inc., New York.
www.crownpublishing.com
www.clarksonpotter.com

CLARKSON POTTER is a trademark and
POTTER with colophon is a registered trademark
of Random House, Inc.

Library of Congress Cataloging-in-Publication Data
Bone, Eugenia.
    Well-Preserved / Eugenia Bone. — 1st ed.
        p.   cm.
    Includes index.
    1. Canning and preserving.   2. Food—Preservation.
I. Title.
TX603.B6577   2009
641.4—dc22   2008040528

ISBN 978-0-307-40524-1

Printed in China

Design by Amy Sly

Page 1: Three-Citrus Marmalade (page 100);
frontispiece: Cherries in Wine (page 48); *page 6:*
Stewed Onions with Marjoram Soup (page 151)

10   9   8   7   6   5   4

First Edition

To Edward Giobbi and Lucille Shannon.
Between his tuna and her crabapple jelly,
I fell in love with canning.

CONTENTS

INTRODUCTION

I always walk to my local farmers' market on Saturdays reciting the mantra "*I will not overbuy, I will not overbuy.*" As much as I love fresh fruits and vegetables, it makes me feel guilty to see them wrinkling and browning and bruising every time I open my fridge. But then I'm at the market, and I smell the strawberries or notice the yellow zucchini blossoms, the tomatoes fragrant as flowers, and the sea scallops cold and fresh off the *Brianna*, the sweet corn a dozen ears for $3, and asparagus? *I love them!*

When my husband sees all the food I cart home, he inevitably gives me the "You need to join a group" look. But within a couple of days I manage to process all that glorious produce into jars and freezer bags, tucked away for future use, preserving the season in all its wonderful freshness and optimism. I want the bounty to go on forever, and in ways both literal and meta-phorical, preserving is, for me, a tactic for capturing time.

Coming from an Italian household, home preserving was always a part of the ebb and flow of the seasons. My dad put up a wide variety of foods—tuna in the late summer, tomatoes in the fall, prosciutto in the winter, as well as hot peppers stuffed with bread crumbs, pickled fava beans, olives, pesto, the must from pressed wine grapes, wild mushrooms. . . . I enjoyed eating it all. But it is one thing to be the recipient of someone else's effort and quite another to do the work yourself. My dad lives in the country. He has a big kitchen, an even bigger garden, and woods teeming with wild things. I live in a rental in Manhattan and am powering through the supermom life, which means I have limited space and less time. Eventually, though, I learned you don't need a big country kitchen, or an orchard out back, to can with enthusiasm. Cities host excellent farmers' markets, and I've chosen the path of small-batch preserving, more inclined to variety than quantity. I've also learned that I do indeed have the time to can, because by putting up small amounts of foods from which I can make subsequent meals, I expend less energy preparing dinner. I can accommodate unexpected guests with ease and flair. All it takes is an inspection of my freezer or my larder—what the husband calls "the bomb shelter."

Ironically, my interest in preserving didn't start at home: it was ignited during my second sophomore year of college. I lived in a ratty railroad flat above Mamoon's Falafel on Bleecker Street in New York City. Probably as an act of charity (I was living on peanut butter and falafel), a friend of my parents', the restaurant critic Jay Jacobs, used to take me to lunch when he was reviewing. We eventually became good friends in our own right, and Jay invited me to brunch at his Upper East Side apartment. All kinds of sophisticates were there, and me, a fairly unpolished twenty-year-old in a plastic miniskirt. I was dazzled—not by the muckety-mucks sipping Corton Charlemagne and trading stock tips, but by the buffet: soft scrambled eggs, golden brioche as

Home-canned tuna

puffy as cumulus clouds, and a curling pile of thinly sliced gravlax, coral colored and opalescent, that was utterly light and creamy. I was smitten. Jay told me he'd made the gravlax a couple days before, that a monkey could make it and I was welcome to the recipe.

That such a marvelous dish could be made at home and stored in my wheezing old refrigerator was a miracle to me. I went back to my apartment, Jay's twenty-something son in tow, where we smoked a joint. While I rhapsodized about cured fish, imagining my own brilliant brunches, he swooned and fell off the edge of my platform bed. That and other distractions ensured it would be another six years before I actually made the recipe.

My canning fixation came into full flower when I was eight months pregnant with my second child, Mo. I had gone into the nesting stage. For some women that means buying burp cloths or stenciling borders on the nursery wall, but for me it was an obsession with preserving. Somehow I just got it into my head that with two small children I'd be housebound for months and we would all likely starve. When I told my father that I wanted to can, it was like encountering a fellow smoker on the sidewalk—he was my co-conspirator—and we put up twenty pints of tomatoes that first year. My fears of domestic incarceration passed soon after my son was born, but the pleasure of having those tomatoes in the cupboard stuck with me.

Over the course of the next few years Dad also taught me how to preserve in oil, how to pickle, and how to cure, but I think my most cherished canning recipe from him was pressure-canned tuna fish. We used to summer in Provincetown, Massachusetts, when I was a kid, and every August Dad would go to the docks pulling a child's red wagon and roll home a tremendous two-hundred-pound tuna that he'd bought off the pier and gutted there, chucking the chum into the bay among screeching gulls. Dad flopped the big silver fish, round as a barrel, into the only bathtub in the house, where he salted it and soaked it in cold running water. For two days the fish bled in the tub. It was fascinating, but in my self-conscious pubescence I found it intimidating to use the toilet with that big fish so close, its round eye staring glassily at the showerhead.

When the tuna was clean, Dad cleared off the dinner table and butchered the meat. The best part—the fatty belly meat—we ate fresh; the rest he shoved into half-pint jars, covered in oil, and pressure-canned. Cases of pink meat glistened in jars, aging under the couches, until we went home to New York. It seemed an impossible feat, the work of a titan canner. And then, about five years ago, my buddy Beaver (his real moniker: all the Truax boys were named after small mammals) got a connection to a fisherman in Montauk who delivered the goods: twenty pounds of yellowtail caught just twenty-four hours earlier. After numerous conference calls with my father, we canned it up. I've been canning tuna ever since, albeit smaller amounts of fish I buy retail. I kind of miss the tuna in the tub, but every fall I preserve the memory in a jar.

I also freeze as a means of preserving, though the capacity of my freezer was, until recently, strained by a third ice cube tray. One August, however, while hanging out at our cabin in Colorado, we stumbled across a mother lode of porcini mushrooms and chanterelles, as big as teacups. I sautéed the mushrooms until they released their liquid, then froze them in their own broth and lugged them—about thirty pounds' worth—back to New York. There I was faced with a dilemma. Even if I defrosted my permafrosted freezer, I would be hard-pressed to fit thirty pounds of anything inside. That day the husband and I went to the local electronics emporium. Today I may be the only person in fabulous SoHo with a chest freezer.

During the course of the year I put up a wide variety of foods that I use in multiple dishes, from cured bacon (ridiculously easy to make and much tastier than commercial) for frisée salad with lardons and poached eggs or savory chicken Canzanese with bacon, garlic, sage, and rosemary; to Foriana sauce, a combination of walnuts, pine nuts, raisins, garlic, and oregano that I use to stuff clams and thick-cut pork chops. I preserve all sorts of things: smoked chicken breasts for salads and sandwiches; pickled cauliflower to make a romping vegetable dish with tomatoes and black olives; and brandied figs to cook into sweet, rich sauces for quail and duck or stir into mashed yams. In the fall I can tuna and, after allowing it to season for six months, use it in pasta dishes, composed salads, or vitello tonnato, all excellent in the spring. I also make sweet concoctions, like grated apples flavored with warm pie spices, which I dump into a crust to make a pie, or roll into a crisp strudel, and from the leftover juices, icy apple-pie-flavored granita; and Concord grape and walnut conserve, which I use to make a tart or mix with chocolate, stuff into ravioli, and fry.

Often I will combine two canned goods in a dish, though I have resisted the inclination to cross-reference the recipes in the book. But ideally, you can cross-pollinate these recipes using multiple goods that you have preserved. In fact, just thinking about these recipes brings to mind new, delicious combinations. How about this? Spiced Apples (page 89) and brandied fig tart (page 59), Spaghettini with Tuna (page 208) and a dollop of Green Olive Tapenade (page 71), or a Cobb salad with Smoked Chicken Breasts (page 198) and home-cured Bacon (page 193)? Chicken Canzanese (page 197) would be great garnished with a mound of Mushroom Duxelles (page 185). Actually, so would Duck Breast with Brandied Fig Sauce (page 61). Yeah, baby.

This morning, before I sat down to finish this introduction, I went to the farmers' market. It's early fall, just beginning to cool off, and the red peppers are in, cheap and magnificent. So are the tomatoes. I load up. Heading home I couldn't resist an earthy pound or two of hen-of-the-woods mushrooms at the wild craft booth and then purchased two quarts of opulently purple Concord grapes, because I just had to. If I could have carried it, I would have bought a peck of sunny Golden Delicious apples as well. They smelled so good.

About 25 percent of all households in the United States can, the majority of them in the country, and for all sorts of reasons: necessity, pleasure, health. (A serious canner friend of mine from Routt County, Colorado, told me a story about a mortician in her town. "He said in the past morticians used to have to get a body into the earth real quick, but nowadays a human body will hold for two weeks due to all the commercial preservatives he's eaten." Lovely.) Home canning reduces your carbon footprint, increases the quality of your dining experience, and provides a sense of independence from the industrial food complex—all excellent reasons to get into it. Plus, it's very relaxing and cheaper than psychotherapy.

But for me the canning experience provides something beyond good health and convenience and political expression: because it takes time and care to accomplish, the craft of home canning slows down my relationship with food. Preserving is not about immediate satisfaction (for that, eat the cherries fresh). It's about anticipation. And in that sense it's an act of optimism. Yes, the world will be here in two weeks when my marinated artichokes have finished seasoning. And no, life is not slipping past unacknowledged and unrevered.

In my bomb shelter there are a couple of jars of last spring's pickled asparagus. I canned them the same day my young son told me how much he loved it when the trees had blossoms and baby leaves on them at the same time.

You see, I'd almost forgotten that.

ALL ABOUT CANNING

I think the reason more people don't can is ultimately that they're scared of botulism poisoning. Understandable. But if you educate yourself on the simple science underlying safe canning, it will put those fears in perspective and open the door to really cool cooking experiences. In a nutshell, preserving is about prolonging the shelf life of foods by killing or neutralizing the agents that would otherwise cause them to spoil. That is accomplished by freezing, heat, and/or creating an environment that is unsustainable for spoiling agents.

So, what are the spoilers? Food companies that would have you buy their canned goods rather than prepare your own have been very effective at spooking people about spoilers. Let's look at the facts.

ENZYMES cause decomposition. They occur naturally in all living things. Enzymes are most active between 85°F and 120°F, which is why refrigeration slows down decomposition. You can destroy enzymes by heating up their host (the food) to 140°F (boiling at sea level is 212°F, which is why blanching is usually all that is called for prior to freezing).

MOLDS—that white fuzz that grows on leftovers in your fridge—are fungi that spring from microscopic spores that alight on foods. There is good mold and bad mold. Good mold is introduced into foods, like blue cheeses, or anticipated eagerly, as in the "noble rot" of late-harvest wine grapes. Bad mold is not edible. Molds cannot grow in freezing temperatures, but they can survive and will start to bloom from 50°F to 100°F. They can be destroyed at temperatures from 140°F to 190°F. The higher the temperature, the faster they will die.

YEASTS are another type of fungi that cause fermentation. Again, certain yeasts are introduced into food deliberately, as in bread and beer. Other yeasts sour foods unappetizingly. Like molds, yeasts cannot grow in freezing temperatures, although they can survive and will start to bloom at temperatures between 50°F and 100°F. They can be destroyed at temperatures from 140°F to 190°F. Again, like molds, the higher the temperature, the faster yeasts will die.

BACTERIA are the big bugaboo in canning. Some can thrive in temperatures that would kill yeasts and molds. And in certain foods, types of bacteria may thrive that can cause paralysis and even death. So, for those foods (very few of which are used in this book), the temperature must be brought up to 240°F and held there for a specified time. This is hotter than can be achieved with a water bath, and so the food must be canned under pressure using a stovetop pressure canner.

There are two classes of bacteria: relatively fragile germs like Salmonellae that live in frozen food, but activate above 45°F. They can be killed at 140°F (well below boiling) if held at that temperature for a prescribed amount of time, and die quicker at higher temperatures. Other bacteria, like Staphylococcus and *Clostridium botulinum,* the bacterium that causes botulism, may be inactive at lower temperatures, but to kill them you need to expose them to a high temperature: 240°F for a sustained length of time, obtainable only with a pressure canner.

Knowing which preservation technique to use is key to producing a food that is both safe and tasty. This book is composed of recipes using six different food preservation techniques, all simple, all safe. Following, you'll find a synopsis of each technique, how it works and why it's safe, and the types of foods it's best suited for. Very detailed descriptions of the different preservation methods will follow.

- **WATER BATH CANNING**

  When foods in glass jars are processed in boiling water for a prescribed amount of time, the heat generated by the boiling water pushes the air out of the tissues of the foods and jar, creating a vacuum seal. It also sterilizes the food and jar. This technique is safe for foods that have a pH (acidity) of 4.5 or less, primarily fruits, and for fruits and vegetables with the appropriate addition of acid, such as vinegar. This process kills all spoilers except the botulism bacterium, but the bacterium cannot thrive in a pH environment of 4.5 or less.

- **PICKLING**

  Pickling is the process of preserving foods in a high-acid solution in which spoilers cannot grow. This state of high acidity is achieved in two ways: by means of salt and with vinegar (though when you pickle with vinegar, you usually add salt as well). The pickled foods in this book are preserved for shelf life by water bath canning. This process is good for low-acid vegetables (pH 4.6 and up).

- **PRESSURE CANNING**

  You will need a pressure canner to process foods under pressurized heat for a prescribed amount of time. Steam builds up in the airtight cavity of the pressure canner, accomplishing the same thing as a water bath canner but at much higher temperatures. This technique kills all spoilers. Period. Pressure canning is used when processing low-acid foods (pH 4.6 and higher), primarily vegetables without added acid, meat, and fish.

- **FREEZING**

  Bringing raw, semicooked, or thoroughly cooked food to a temperature between 0°F and 32°F slows the metabolism of foods and the spoilers that may live on them. Spoilers are not destroyed, but they don't bloom either. With proper defrosting and prompt cooking and/or heating, spoilers in foods that have been frozen will never amount to anything. This process is effective for a large variety of foods.

- **PRESERVING IN OIL**

  In this process, foods are covered in an impenetrable layer of oil and refrigerated. Foods that are cooked—which kills many spoilers—before being covered in oil and refrigerated last longer than raw foods that have been covered in oil and refrigerated. As air cannot penetrate olive oil, it acts as a seal between the foodstuff and the environment, forestalling the growth of spoilers longer than simple refrigeration. The downside of preserving in oil, besides the fact that it doesn't hold food for terribly long, is that the food becomes saturated with oil and so is useful only in recipes to which you would have added oil anyway.

- **CURING AND SMOKING**

  Curing is the art of permeating food with salt via a dry cure (combining the food with dry salt) or a brine (soaking the food in salt and water combined). Salt urges water from cells, which dehydrates the flesh; as spoilers need moisture to grow, salt-cured foods provide an inhospitable environment for microbes. Likewise, salt enters and dehydrates the microbes themselves, wreaking havoc on a spoiler's ability to survive. Cured foods last for weeks in the refrigerator. Smoking (inundating a food with hot or cold smoke) is often executed in conjunction with curing. Smoking adds flavor, kills microorganisms through heat, and extends the life of the product. Curing is an excellent preservative process for proteins.

I used a variety of sources to learn about these preservation techniques. I took Master Food Safety Advisor Volunteer Training offered by Colorado State University Extension. All state universities are obliged to provide a free educational outlet for the public whose tax dollars support them. Called the Cooperative State Research, Education, and Extension Service (CSREES), their mission is to "advance knowledge for agriculture, the environment, human health and well-being, and communities." To find the nearest agency, search State University of (your state) Extension Office or Cooperative Extension Program (plus your state). You can also call your state university. Extension offices are valuable resources that every canner should cultivate.

I learned a lot about the science of preserving from researching these state university websites and checking a plethora of websites and blogs by chefs and home cooks, food scientists and artisans (trying to separate the wheat from the chaff was an education in itself) and by reading books. Lots of books. My favorites are *Putting Food By* by Ruth Hertzberg, Beatrice Vaughan, and Janet Greene (Stephen Greene Press, 1973); *Stocking Up* by Carol Hupping and the staff at the Rodale Food Center (Fireside, 1986), and *Ball Complete Book of Home Preserving* edited by Judi Kingry and Lauren Devine (Robert Rose Inc., 2006) for general canning recipes and guidelines; the brilliant *Cooking by Hand* by Paul Bertolli (Clarkson Potter, 2003) and *Charcuterie* by Michael Ruhlman and Brian Polcyn (W. W. Norton and Company, 2005) for curing and smoking; and *The Joy of Pickling* by Linda Ziedrich (Harvard Common Press, 1998), an unbelievably good resource. Additionally, I consulted with CSU Extension specialists Marisa Bunning, PhD, and Mary Schroeder, MS, RD, for additional food safety expertise.

In the case of the canned recipes, I generally used USDA—approved recipes, altering only those ingredients that did not affect the pH or overall volume of the product. I also tested the pH of the finished product: I allowed the product to rest for two to three weeks, made a slurry (using only distilled water where necessary), and tested the slurry with a pH meter. (To buy your own meter, contact Cole-Parmer Instrument Company at 847-549-7600 or coleparmer.com.)

That said, you can't play fast and loose with the water-bath- and pressure-canned recipes in this book (have your way with the dishes in which they are used). Follow the recipes and you'll be fine. Please don't make substitutions and don't adjust quantities of ingredients unless you are willing to go whole hog and figure out the pH of the recipes yourself and how long they should be processed. Likewise, be wise about altitude adjustments. All the recipes in this book are adjusted for sea level. When water bath canning, add one minute of processing time for each 1,000 feet above sea level if the processing time is 20 minutes or less and 2 minutes for every 1,000 feet if the processing time is more than 20 minutes. When pressure canning, add ½ pound pressure for every 1,000 feet above sea level, but don't change the processing time. When blanching vegetables prior to freezing, add 1 minute of blanching time if you live above 5,000 feet.

I highly recommend that you read the detailed descriptions of the preserving techniques that follow as you need them. The more knowledge you have, the more confident you will be.

WATER BATH CANNING

My first forays into preserving were water-bath-canned foods. I started with crabapple jelly, a favorite from my childhood, and tomatoes. Jams and jellies are very satisfying to make, but unless you are a dedicated breakfast eater (and I am not—some leftover sushi around 10:00 A.M. is perfect for me), there's only so much you can do with them. However, once I started adding alcohol or balsamic vinegar, I found I could use my jams in more savory options. Pickles came later. But tomatoes! *That* was a revelation. I just couldn't believe how easy it was to put up a food that, when used in recipes, improved the quality of my cooking more than any other single factor (including a stint at cooking school).

WHAT IS WATER BATH CANNING?

Water bath canning is a way of processing high-acid foods like fruits and pickled vegetables for long-term storage. High-acid food is packed into clean or sterile glass jars with metal bands and new lids, and the jars are boiled in water for a prescribed amount of time. Successful water bath canning is composed of two simple stages: killing elements that cause spoilage of foods (enzymes, mold, yeasts, and bacteria) and establishing a sealed container where new elements cannot be introduced. These conditions, combined with the high acidity of the food within the jar, ensure that harmful microorganisms do not develop and the food is safe to store on the shelf. Because spoilers, including *Clostridium botulinum,* the bacterium that causes botulism, cannot develop in a high-acid environment, foods that have a pH of 4.5 or lower are safe to water bath can.

Canning works like this: The high heat drives out the air that is within the tissue of the foods as well as the air that was trapped during the packing process. This creates a vacuum, which makes the rubberized flange on the lid suck down onto the jar rim and create a seal. After you remove the jars from the water bath and allow them to cool, you will hear a popping noise. That's the sound of the suck and seal. The cooling part of water bath processing is important: the rubber seal will be soft coming out of the water bath and it needs to stiffen up to complete the process.

HOW DOES WATER BATH CANNING WORK?

Each recipe in this book tells you how long the jar must be boiled to kill spoilers and create a vacuum seal. You will notice that the boiling times vary for different foods and different jar sizes. There are three reasons for this:

1. Different foods have different densities, which affects how long it takes for the heat to penetrate the food thoroughly and subsequently kill the spoilers and create a vacuum in the jar.
2. The length of time needed to process a food also depends on the acidity (natural or added) of the food you are canning. That's because the pH, or acidity, of a food affects the ability of spoilers to thrive: the higher the acid content of the food, the less boiling time needed to kill spoilers.
3. Another factor in judging how long a product must boil is how large a jar you are processing. For example, it takes longer for the heat to reach temperature in the center of the food in a quart jar than a pint jar.

WHAT DIFFERENCE DOES IT MAKE HOW LONG I BOIL JARS IN A WATER BATH?

Any food with a pH of 4.5 or lower can be canned safely in a water bath, as can food that has been acidified to a pH rating of 4.5 or less. This is because high-acid foods like fruits don't need to be heated beyond 212°F, the boiling point, to destroy spoilers or render them inert at sea level. (Tomatoes are just high enough in acid to can in a water bath, especially if they aren't too ripe— the sweetness of a tomato occurs when it ripens and the acid in it turns to sugar. The USDA rec- ommends adding lemon juice or citric acid to ensure there is enough acidity to let you can them safely.) Low-acid foods, like vegetables without added vinegar, meat, and fish, need to be sub- jected to greater heat (240°F) to destroy spoilers, and so they must be pressure-canned. (See page 28 for an overview of how to pressure can low-acid foods.)

WHICH FOODS ARE SAFE TO WATER BATH CAN?

Fruit, like lemons, have a lot of natural acid and can be safely water bath canned. Vegetables are low in natural acid and so must be pickled for water bath canning—meaning you add acid (usually vinegar) to the food and then can it. Meats and fish are at the lowest end of the scale: you can't add enough acid to water bath can them safely and have them still be edible (so you would use another method of preserving). For the pH values of various foods, check out http://vm.cfsan.fda.gov and select "Acidified and Low Acid Canned Foods," then "Approximate pH of Foods and Food Products."

HOW DO I KNOW HOW MUCH ACID A FOOD HAS?

The added acids used in this book are bottled lemon juice and vinegar with 5 percent acidity. The reason you must use bottled lemon juice rather than fresh is to ensure consistency in the acidity. Fresh lemons will vary in acidity. The recipes don't call for salad vinegars, because salad vinegars may have sediment in them or a strong taste or color that will inhibit optimum results.

There are four steps: (1) Prepare the food. (2) Sterilize the jars if the processing time is 10 minutes or less. (3) Pack the jars with the food and wipe the rims. (4) Process the jars in boiling water. That's it.

WHAT ARE THE STEPS TO WATER BATH CANNING?

Cleanliness is *important*, but you don't need to be paranoid. It's really more a matter of common sense: Don't wash foods in water you wouldn't drink. Wash your hands before beginning to can. You don't have to presterilize any of your equipment, like the pot you heat the foods in, or the spoon you stir with, or the tongs you use to remove jars from the hot water, but I recommend resting the ladle or spoon you use to fill the jars in the boiling water for a few minutes. It's not necessary, just a good precaution. (Watch out: the handle will get hot.)

HOW CRUCIAL IS CLEANLINESS?

I use glass Ball or Kerr jars, with screw-on bands and lids, which are easily ordered online (homecanning.com). You can reuse the glass jars and the metal bands—the bands if they aren't rusty or dented, the jars if they aren't chipped or cracked—but you must buy new lids (a flat metal disk with a rubberized flange) for every new sealing. Lids are sold with new jars and in separate packs of twelve.

WHAT KIND OF EQUIPMENT DO I NEED?

To sterilize jars, and then to can them in a water bath, I use a big pasta pot with a tight-fitting lid and a rack. The rack allows the water to circulate around the jars. Also, without a rack the jars will rattle like crazy while they are boiling and may break, and the sound is nerve-wracking. The pot must be deep enough to cover the jars with water by a couple of inches and then still have an additional couple of inches so the boiling water doesn't erupt all over your stove. You don't want to have to turn the water down to avoid spilling, as a rolling boil produces the temperature you're after.

I use a *jar-lifter* or *tongs* to pull the sterilized jars and bands out of the water. But tongs aren't the best tool for pulling filled, processed jars out of the boiling water, as the jars are heavy and very hot. (And you don't want to leave the jars in the water bath until they are cool enough to handle or the foods will become overprocessed. In the case of some products, this can lead to colorless or wrinkled foods.) I suggest buying a jar-lifter, a cheap, nifty piece of equipment that allows you to grasp and withdraw the hot jars firmly. (If you buy your jars online, you will see a selection of canning equipment for sale too. There's a canning set made by Ball that's full of groovy doodads that make canning easier, though none are essential.) Otherwise, dump out half of the boiling water once processing is complete and lift the jars out using an *oven mitt*.

For pickling, you need a *glass, stainless-steel, ceramic, or enamel bowl* for the brining stage, as vinegar corrodes iron, copper, brass, and galvanized metal (which is made with zinc—you shouldn't use galvanized metal pots for any type of cooking).

A *candy thermometer* that goes up to 220°F is useful in ensuring your marmalade has reached the right temperature. Otherwise, the recipes provide tests you can do by eye.

Have a *roll of paper towels* on hand for wiping rims.

DO I NEED TO STERILIZE THE FOOD?

Not if the food is processed in a water bath for more than 10 minutes. Nonetheless, in most of these recipes the food is sterilized during its cooking period prior to canning or it is significantly acidified (thus rendering spoilers inert) by pickling or fermentation. However, should you ever be worried about the safety of your preserved foods after they have been processed, remove the food from the jars prior to using in a recipe and boil the food in a pan for at least 10 minutes (plus 1 minute for each additional 1,000 feet above sea level). This will sterilize your food by destroying any molds, yeasts, or bacteria, including potential botulism toxin, that may be present.

HOW DO I STERILIZE GLASS JARS AND BANDS?

You need to start with sterilized jars only if the processing time in the recipe is 10 minutes or less, the amount of time it takes to sterilize a jar. Sterilization will happen simultaneously with the water bath processing if the processing time is longer than 10 minutes. To sterilize jars and bands, you simply place them in a large pot with a rack on the bottom, cover with water, and bring that water to a rapid boil for 10 minutes. I remove jars from boiling water with tongs. Ideally, you'll fill the jars when they are dry but still hot, but I never get the timing right. So I just keep the jars boiling until my food is almost ready to be packed, then remove the jars and shake out the excess water. I let them dry for a minute or two, then fill them. You don't want to let the jars dry out so long that they cool, because then you've undermined the sterilization, giving little floating microorganisms a chance to alight on a surface that isn't too hot for them. Likewise, don't dry the jars with a towel (it's not sterile). There is no way to ensure 100 percent sterility, but it's really okay, because you will be processing these jars in a boiling water bath, which is going to kill most everything all over again, as well as create an airless environment. You do not need to sterilize new lids (too much heat can damage the rubberized flange). Simply simmer the lids in a small pan of hot water to soften the rubberized flange.

The food is packed into the sterilized jars up to 1 inch from the top of the glass. This layer of air between the top of your food and the inside of the lid is called the *headspace*. This space is there to allow for a small increase in the volume of the product or for the foods to bubble as they are canned. If you don't leave enough headspace, some of the food might be forced out of the jars with the air, which could ruin your seal. Too much headspace can cause a buildup of pressure inside the jar, leading to cracks in the glass. Too much headspace can also cause discoloration of foods or a seal failure, as it would take a longer processing time to force out more air than the recipes call for. Filling the jars just to the point of the rim rings on the glass allows adequate headspace for all the recipes in this book. Use a damp paper towel to wipe the rim of the jar—all of the parts that the band will screw on to—of any food that may have dribbled on while you were packing it. This is important because little sticky bits of food can inhibit the seal, and you need a good strong seal to ensure that no air gets into your jars. It doesn't matter if the body of the jar has dribbles clinging to it: that will wash off during the water bath processing. (If you want clean, shiny jars when you remove them from the water bath, add ½ teaspoon of distilled white vinegar to the water.) Don't screw on the bands too tightly. They should be screwed down until "finger-tip" tight, just tight enough to close with your fingertips, not cranked with your palm. This is because you want all the air in the jar to be able to escape during the water bath processing.

HOW DO I PACK THE JARS?

The jars are placed in a pot and covered with water. I often reuse the pot of water in which I sterilized the jars—your main concern here is to avoid placing boiling-hot jars in cold water and vice versa, or you run the risk of cracking the glass. The jars need to be submerged under a couple of inches of water. This is important because you want to make sure the entire jar comes up to the temperature of the water surrounding it. Since water boils at 212°F at sea level, the microorganisms in high-acid foods are going to expire or be rendered inert. It also sterilizes the inner parts of the jar a second time, in case any spoilers made their way in while you were packing.

HOW DO I WATER BATH CAN THE JARS?

Once the processing is complete, remove the jars from the water bath and allow them to cool on a rack or dish towel for 6 to 8 hours. You can then remove the bands and check the seals. You don't need the bands if your seals were successful. Indeed, leaving the bands off is best, because that way you will know if a seal breaks or goes bad over time. I screw the bands back on for shipping or otherwise carrying the jars about.

HOW DO I KNOW THE JARS HAVE SEALED?

Everybody worries about this one too much: it is obvious when the seal isn't good. You can check the seal by tapping on the lid after the jar has been processed and is cool. It will be taut and pulled down toward the inside of the jar. A lid that bounces when you press on it is either not cool yet, and so hasn't created its vacuum, or has an insufficient seal. The ultimate test is to unscrew the bands and, with your thumb and middle finger, grasp the jar by the edge of the lid and lift. If the seal is good, you will be able to lift the jar by the seal alone.

WHAT IF I LIVE ABOVE SEA LEVEL?

You need to add 1 minute of processing time for every 1,000 feet in altitude. If you live at 3,500 feet, round up to 4,000 and add 4 extra minutes to the processing time in the recipes. You need to make this adjustment because water boils at a lower temperature the higher your altitude. You need to add time to compensate for the reduced heat to create that seal.

HOW DO I STORE MY JARS?

Best is a cool, dark place. Sun will bleach out the jars' contents eventually, and excessive heat may compromise the seals. (By excessive heat I am thinking of scenarios like leaving the jars in the trunk of your car in a sunny parking space for a week.) Canned goods keep for up to a year. That's the official recommendation. Unofficially, I have some pretty old vintages in my pantry that I am saving for special.

PICKLING

I am not an enthusiastic cucumber pickle eater. I pretty much like two kinds: bread-and-butter pickles made into a relish to eat with hamburgers and hot dogs and little sour cornichons to eat with pâté. However, there are many dishes I eat that call for vinegar, as in sausages with cauliflower, and so there was a certain logic in preparing pickled cauliflower: having it on hand meant that instead of adding vinegar when cooking the sausages and then blanching the cauliflower and adding it as well, I could simply dump the contents of my jar over the browned sausage and be done. So besides the pleasure of preserving a food when it is cheap and seasonal—and there is nothing more tempting than a fresh, tight, white head of cauliflower and little more disappointing than watching it brown over the course of a week in the fridge—I have the added satisfaction of knowing all I need to make dinner is to pick up a pound or two of fresh sausages and a bunch of fresh parsley to prepare a delicious (and quick) meal.

So what is pickling? Pickling is the process of preserving foods in a high-acid solution, either by adding vinegar or naturally by means of fermentation. Spoilers cannot grow in a high-acid environment. This state of high acidity is achieved in two ways: by means of salt and with vinegar (though when you pickle with vinegar, you add salt as well). Let's look at salt pickling first.

PICKLING WITH SALT

Pickling with salt falls into two categories: dry salt and brined. The dry salt method combines dry salt with vegetables in quantities above what you would add for seasoning purposes. Liquid (watery juices) is pulled from the vegetables, and this liquid combines with the salt to create a brine—a salty, watery solution. With the premade brine method, a vegetable is placed in a combination of salt and water. In both cases the vegetables are covered in brine for a prescribed amount of time. In this submerged, airless state (below the brine line), the vegetables ferment. Fermentation is the process by which the natural bacteria in the foods convert the sugars into lactic acid. Lactic acid is a natural preservative: depending on its strength, microorganisms will not grow in lactic acid because of its low pH (high acidity). As a result, low-acid foods like cabbage can be canned safely in a water bath canner and stored on the shelf for up to a year once fermentation is complete. Lactic acid also supplies that yummy sour taste—hence the name *sauerkraut.*

PICKLING WITH VINEGAR

Pickling with vinegar is a much quicker process. In vinegar pickling, the vegetable does not ferment. Usually, the vegetable rests for a short time in a brine (to add crispness and flavor), is drained, often brought to a boil in a vinegar solution, packed into jars, covered in the remaining hot vinegar solution, and water bath canned for long-term preservation. The acetic acid in vinegar brings up the acidity of the vegetable to a point where no microorganisms can thrive. Acetic acid, by the way, is flavorless and colorless. When a recipe calls for vinegar that is 5 percent acid, that means the vinegar is 5 percent acetic acid.

WHEN MAKING PICKLED FOODS, IT IS CRITICAL THAT YOU USE VERY FRESH INGREDIENTS. If you start out to make sauerkraut with an old soft cabbage, your end product will be mushy. Basically, crisp into the brining pot means crisp out of the brining pot. (And this is true of all preserving: don't put up foods that are on their way out. Preserving is not a way to postpone eating something that has been aging in your refrigerator. Rather, preserving is capturing a food's optimum freshness in time.)

THE ONLY INGREDIENTS NECESSARY TO PICKLING ARE THE FOOD YOU ARE PLANNING TO PICKLE, EITHER SALT OR VINEGAR OR A COMBINATION, AND WATER. Salt is key, and it matters which kind you use. Use pickling or canning salt or kosher salt. Pickling salt (sometimes called *canning and pickling salt*) is pure granulated salt. It is free of anticaking agents, which can cause the pickling liquid to turn cloudy. Table salt with iodide (iodized salt) is not a good choice. It won't hurt you, but it will undermine the appearance of your pickles, as the additives do not dissolve completely. I often use kosher salt because it just tastes saltier to me. However, kosher salt has large crystals, which do not dissolve as quickly as pickling salt. When making a premade brine, you have to either heat kosher salt and water together to ensure the salt is totally dissolved or combine the salt and water together in a bowl and swish it around until all the crystals are dissolved. Another factor regarding kosher salt is volume. The large crystals of kosher salt take up less space in your measuring spoon than the smaller pickling salt crystals.

The pickling recipes in this book call for pickling salt. If you want to substitute kosher, you need to add a bit more kosher salt than the recipe calls for. I find it effective to add heaping tablespoons of kosher salt where I would add a level tablespoon of pickling salt: not very scientific, but it works for me.

Sea salt is produced by the evaporation of salt water. It comes in fine and coarse textures and a variety of colors. The problem with pickling with sea salt is consistency. Because it is an unregulated product, you just don't know what minerals are in there or how they are going to affect your pickling. Disregarding the fact that it is expensive, sea salt is not the best choice for pickling. Rather, on the occasions when I indulge myself with one of those lovely jars of pink sea salt, I use it to garnish foods.

Water is also important. During fermentation, hard water (mineral-rich water) and heavily chlorinated water can interfere with the formation of lactic acid. You can tell you have hard water if it stains the toilet and heavily chlorinated water if it smells like a swimming pool. In this case, you have two options. Either buy distilled water or bring your tap water to a boil for 15 minutes, cover, and then let it sit for 24 hours. You will detect a scum on top and sediment on the bottom. Skim off the scum and pour the water into another container, leaving the sediment behind. However, if your water is good to drink, it is good to pickle with.

And finally, vinegar. Again, it's all about that 5 percent acidity. I use Heinz distilled white vinegar, cider vinegar, and white wine vinegar. Distilled white vinegar is made from grain alcohol. It is clear, pungent, and flavorless. Because of its clarity, distilled white vinegar is preferred when appearance matters, especially when pickling pale vegetables. Cider vinegar is distilled from hard cider (fermented apple juice). It has a light golden color and a softly tart taste. It is milder than distilled white vinegar but causes the vegetables to darken somewhat. White wine vinegar is my favorite, probably owing as much to my Italian heritage as anything else. The taste is fruity and strong. You can try the recipes with malt vinegar, fermented from barley, but avoid rice vinegar, which may not be up to the 5 percent dilution level. Ultimately, you can substitute any vinegar you want, as long as it is 5 percent acidity (or higher) and you use the amount of vinegar called for in the recipes. Just keep in mind the aesthetic element: brown or red vinegars (particularly balsamic and red wine vinegars) will darken your foods.

OTHER INGREDIENTS YOU WILL ENCOUNTER IN PICKLING ARE SUGAR (WHITE AND BROWN), HERBS, SPICES, AND GARLIC. Of these, unrefined sugar is fine to use if you prefer it. Fresh herbs should be just that. Don't use fresh herbs that are browning or slimy. Spices should be fresh too. It's a shame they are so expensive, because the fact is, after a year you should chuck your spices out, as they diminish in flavor. (Just sniff. If you can't smell anything, the spice or dried herb is finito.) You should use aged, cured garlic. While very fresh garlic is a delight to eat, it will discolor during pickling. Garlic that has cured at room temperature for 2 to 3 weeks is best (and that is primarily what you get at the supermarket).

I don't use firming agents (to crisp up vegetables), but for the record, there are two: lime and alum. Lime is calcium hydroxide. Obviously it must be the food-grade product, not that used for agriculture, which is not meant for consumption. In Le Marche, where my dad is from, the large green olive called the Uliva d'Ascoli is cured in lime. Highly prized by the ancient Romans, it is an incredibly sweet, mild olive that the locals peel like an orange and stuff with a meatball mixture and then fry. (See a version of that recipe on page 186.)

Alum is potassium aluminum phosphate or ammonium aluminum sulfate. I know of some canners who lay a grape leaf in the bottom of their jars to firm up their fermented pickles, but I am not one for adding anything to a recipe that I don't have to. I have a very high regard for convenience and simplicity, due to time constraints (New York life and all that).

WHAT KIND OF EQUIPMENT DO I NEED?

For dry salt fermenting the most important item is a 1-gallon stoneware, glass, or food-grade plastic crock. I bought mine—a ceramic crock—at a gourmet kitchen supply store. It has ½-inch-thick walls. I think it was being sold more for decorative purposes—and indeed, I store kitchen utensils in it when I am not using it for fermenting. You'll need a glass, stainless-steel, or ceramic bowl for brining. Avoid all metal bowls besides stainless-steel, as salt and vinegar can react negatively to them. You should also use stainless-steel pots for heating vinegar solutions. Do not use aluminum, copper, brass, galvanized steel, or iron pots for fermenting or heating pickling liquids.

When brining foods, such as cabbage, you must be sure the food stays submerged in the brine. A simple way to accomplish this is to place a food-grade resealable bag filled with extra brine (the salt and water solution) directly atop the food. It is heavy enough to keep the vegetables below the liquid, and if you spring a leak, it's no problem, because only brine will dribble into your crock.

To process jars, you just need the water bath canning setup described on page 20.

THE BASIC STEPS FOR PICKLING

These are: *brining* (which draws water and air out of the vegetables), *packing in jars,* in some recipes *covering with a hot vinegar solution,* and in many recipes *water bath processing.*

Store pickled foods as you would other home-canned products: in a cool, dark place. Pickles should age for about 8 weeks to set the flavor.

I always cheat and open mine early.

PRESSURE CANNING

Lots of people are terrified of pressure canning. And it's true: If you put a steam pressure canner on your stove, crank up the heat, and go to the movies, yes, you will have a problem. If you stay with the task at hand, keeping your eye on the canner during the hour or so it is active, and moderating the heat to the extent necessary, you will end up with beautifully preserved foods.

Pressure canning is the process by which foods (in glass jars) are brought to a high heat (240°F or above) for a predetermined amount of time, obliterating any spoiler that might be alive in the foods and preserving the foods for up to a year.

SO WHAT IS PRESSURE CANNING?

Low-acid foods—specifically anything that has a pH of 4.6 or higher—have to be pressure canned. That includes all vegetables (except tomatoes), meat, and fish. These foods don't have enough natural acid to retard the growth of *Clostridium botulinum,* the bacterium that causes botulism, once the food is processed and in an airless environment. *Clostridium botulinum* thrives in an anaerobic, wet, low-acid, warm environment. To process low-acid foods without adding acid, you must bring the bacterium up to a high enough heat to kill it. Since you can't achieve those kinds of temperatures in a boiling water bath, you must pressure can.

WHAT KINDS OF FOODS HAVE TO BE PRESSURE CANNED?

You pressure can in a steam pressure canner. This is a heavy pot with a lid that can be locked and a pressure gauge that determines the amount of pressure per square inch (psi) within the pot. A pressure canner lid has three to four parts, depending on the model: a gauge, whether dial or weight, that controls pressure; a safety lock or plug, which won't let you open the lid prematurely (before the canner is safely depressurized); and a steam vent (different types are a petcock and safety valve or a weight on the vent), a pipe that, when open, allows steam to escape from the canner. When the steam vent is closed, either by capping it with a weight or flipping it to its closed position, steam can build up pressure in the canner. The steam vent will be forced open if too much steam builds up in the canner. And finally, in some models, a gasket, which is a rubber ring between the lid and pot that ensures an airtight seal.

WHAT KIND OF EQUIPMENT DO I NEED?

THERE ARE A VARIETY OF PRESSURE CANNERS ON THE MARKET (these are not to be confused with pressure cookers or slow cookers). Two dependable companies are Presto and All American. Pressure canners come in a variety of sizes, from the smallest, which can hold 4 quart jars, to large canners, which can hold 7 quart jars. There are two modern styles

Eugenia with jars and her 4-quart All American pressure canner (*right*)

of locking mechanism on the lid: thumb nuts, which are tightened by hand, and slide closures, which slide into a locking position. The two types of closure work equally well, although the slide closure may give the beginner more confidence, as there is no question of whether the lid is on tightly enough. Inside the lid of some canners is a rubber gasket that helps create an airtight seal between the lid and the pot. Gaskets age, of course, and may need to be replaced periodically. You need to check it before each use to be sure it isn't cracked or torn.

There are two types of pressure gauge: the weighted gauge and the dial gauge. A weighted gauge is a weight with three settings—5 pounds, 10 pounds, and 15 pounds—or three separate weights that fit over the steam vent on the lid. The 5-pound setting is used for pressure cooking only, as 5 pounds (psi) is not enough pressure to preserve. Ten pounds of pressure is applied at sea level, and 15 pounds of pressure is used at altitudes above 1,000 feet. This is because the higher the altitude, the lower the atmospheric pressure. You compensate for this discrepancy by adding pressure in the canner. The smallest canner I know of, a Presto 8-quart cooker and canner (that's the total interior volume, not the size and amount of jars that can be processed), has a one-piece weighted gauge set at 15 pounds of pressure that can be used only at altitudes below 3,000 feet, limiting its usefulness. I don't recommend you get one to make the recipes in this or any other book. Weighted gauges don't need to be calibrated.

Dial gauges are just that: a pointer indicates on a scale exactly how much pressure is in the canner. Dial gauges are nice because of the confidence factor—you know what's going on in there. However, dial gauges need to be tested every year or so to ensure they remain accurate. To test a dial gauge, take the lid of your canner to your state university Extension office and have it tested against a master gauge. It is not uncommon for a dial gauge to stray up or down by a pound or two. Up is not a problem when it comes to safety, but you don't want to be canning at less pressure than is required. You can't recalibrate a dial gauge; you just bring up the pressure (by applying more heat) to compensate for the psi you are off. So, if you find out your dial gauge is off by 2 pounds, you need to process succotash at 12 pounds rather than 10 pounds. If it goes off by more than 2 pounds, however, you should replace the gauge.

In the base or pot of the canner is a rack, sometimes two so you can process two layers of jars at once. These racks are just steel disks with holes in them.

I HAVE AN ELECTRIC STOVE. IS THAT AN ISSUE? Not if you have a burner style, although you must use the large burners: if the pot overhangs the burner by more than 2 inches, you won't generate enough heat to do the job. Likewise, if your canner has a rounded or ridged bottom, it won't pick up enough heat on an electric stove, so keep that in mind when buying a canner: there are canners made to accommodate electric, particularly ceramic-top, stoves. Pressure canners, like water bath canners, are heavy, and pressure canning requires a lot of heat over time. Some ceramic-top stoves have a built-in sensor that lowers the heat if the output is too high. This is a drag, because if your pressure drops, you have to stop timing, bring it back up to pressure, and then begin timing again. If this happens numerous times during the 60 to 100 minutes that you are canning, you'll go crazy, and I wouldn't be surprised if you swore off pressure canning forever. My advice, if you have a ceramic-top stove (which I do), is to get a small canner indicated for use with electric stoves (which I did).

HERE'S HOW TO PRESSURE CAN

You don't have to sterilize jars in anticipation of pressure canning, because the pressure canning process will be doing that job for you. Just clean them well. *Fill your jars with food* (leaving 1 inch of headspace) and release any air bubbles that are trapped in the jar with a utensil like a plastic knife. *Wipe the rims* (if you are processing meat or fish, add a little distilled white vinegar to your towel to remove any grease), *set on the lids,* and *screw on the bands* fingertip tight. *Place the jars on the rack* in the canner. *Add 2 to 3 inches of water* (to create the steam). It's okay to eyeball the amount. If you want shiny jars, add ½ teaspoon of distilled white vinegar to the water. *Lock on the lid. Leave the weighted gauge off the vent* or *open the petcock* (your canner instructions will identify it—there's an open and a closed position). *Turn up the heat.* This will bring the water to a boil and produce steam. Steam will come out of the steam vent. This is good. *Allow the steam vent to let off steam for about 10 minutes* to clear. After 10 minutes, either *put the petcock in the closed position and start watching your dial gauge* or *place the weight gauge over the steam vent* at the proper poundage (10 or 15 pounds, depending on your altitude). If you are using a dial gauge, add ½ pound of psi for every 1,000 feet in elevation higher than 1,000 feet above sea level. So, if you live at 3,000 feet, you can set your pressure at 12 pounds, 10 pounds for sea level to 1,000 feet, plus ½ pound for each 1,000 feet above that. If you live at 3,500 feet, round up to 4,000. Your local Extension office will be hip to the psi of your particular area.

If you are using a dial gauge, start to turn down the heat a bit when the gauge reaches 2 pounds of pressure less than your target, so you don't have to turn the heat down to settle at the pressure you want. With a weight gauge, the weight will begin to rock when it achieves the right pressure. You'll hear a rattle, then a pause: a rattle, then a pause. That's what you want to hear. If it is rattling constantly, the heat is a bit high. If it hardly ever rattles, with minutes between rattles, your heat is a bit low. Adjust the heat accordingly. You can't cheat and increase the pressure to shorten the time, because how long a food is under pressure is as important as the pressure under which it is canned. If the pressure drops, turn up the heat and bring the pressure back up. Include in your overall timing only the minutes when the pressure is correct. If, for example, you don't know exactly how many minutes your pressure was off target—was it 3 minutes or 5 minutes?—just round up to play it safe, adding 5 minutes to your overall processing time to compensate. In general, be as exact as you can without driving yourself mad. Some steam may escape around the handles at first. It will stop once full pressure is achieved.

Okay, you've processed your food for the prescribed amount of time. What next? You don't want to just turn off the heat and go away for the weekend. You need to hang around until the safety lock pops, indicating that the pressure has decreased to the point where you can safely remove the lid. If you leave your jars in the canner to cool overnight, for example, the jars will overprocess, because it is still hot in the canner even after the pressure is down. Don't try to cool down the canner by running cold water over it, and if you are using an electric stove, slide the canner off the burner, as the burner generates heat after it has been turned off. *When the safety lock releases,* indicating the pressure is down, *remove the vent weight* or weight gauge (or open the petcock). You should remove the weight gauge away from you, as some hot air will come out. Using oven mitts, *open the lid* away from your face.

As in water bath canning, cooling is a continuation of the process, so after waiting for about 10 minutes for the jars to acclimate, *remove the jars* to the countertop and allow them to rest undisturbed until totally cool, 12 to 24 hours.

Check pressure-canned seals the same way you check water-bath-canned seals: visually, by checking to see if the lids are taut and even slightly concave in the center; audibly, by tapping the lid. You want to hear a dull sound, not a ringing one, and the lid should not bounce when you press it in the center with your finger. Remove the rims (they will have loosened up during processing) and grab the jar by the edge of the lid. If it doesn't pull off, your seal is good.

ARE THE SEALS OKAY?

If your seal is not good, which may happen, although it is unlikely, you can reprocess within 24 hours. Should you choose to reprocess, which just means setting up the foods with new lids and processing at the same psi for the same length of time, remember that reprocessing is going to be pretty hard on your food. You can always freeze it, which is less traumatic to the food than repeated pressure canning. Or you can just go ahead and refrigerate it and eat it within the week. Having gone through the process once, these foods will be ready to use in the associated recipes. Pressure-canned goods, like water bath-canned goods, should be stored in a cool, dark place to avoid bleaching by the sun. The foods should be eaten within 1 year for best quality, not including aging time (see specific recipes for more information about that).

SHOULD YOU HAVE AN ANXIETY ATTACK ABOUT YOUR PRESSURE-CANNED FOODS, KNOW THAT YOU CAN ALWAYS EMPTY A JAR OF PRESSURE-CANNED FOOD INTO A POT AND BOIL FOR 10 MINUTES (plus 1 minute for each additional 1,000 feet above sea level). This will destroy any molds, yeasts, or bacteria, including potential botulism toxin, which may be present. Boiling the food in a recipe counts, but you should eat the foods promptly. Once they are out of that jar, their shelf life is restricted to the usual limitations of refrigeration.

On one occasion when all my seals had failed, I couldn't bear to do the work over, so I just put it all in the refrigerator and ate it. It was a batch of 6 pints of gorgeous bluefin tuna I'd gotten from a fishmonger in Long Island. The jars sealed, but the seals were weak—I could easily pop them open. I now know it was because I didn't leave enough headspace in the jars when I packed them (too much oil). Actually, having all that tuna on hand wasn't so bad: it is how I came up with the tuna recipes in this book in the first place. Indeed, I'd like to amend the saying "Necessity is the mother of invention."

So are perishables.

FREEZING

Even though I am now the proud owner of a chest freezer, I still manage to hoard all kinds of treasures long past a reasonable pull date. But every so often I embark on an excavation project, and it never ceases to thrill when I find a forgotten container of Fava Bean Cream (page 175).

WHAT IS FREEZING, AND HOW DOES IT AFFECT FOODS?

Freezing is the process by which food is solidified by being brought to temperatures between 0°F and 32°F, which in turn slows the life cycle of foods and the spoilers that may live on them. Water in the cells of the food crystallizes and, as a result, expands. The slower the freezing process, the larger the ice crystals, which can cause the cell walls of the food to rupture: this is what makes defrosted foods mushy and is most evident in the case of starchy foods, like peas. (That's why when you see a product labeled "flash frozen," it's a good thing.)

AS A RULE, FOODS THAT HAVE A HIGH WATER CONTENT, LIKE LETTUCE AND CELERY, DON'T FREEZE WELL. The more water in the vegetable, the more ice crystals, the more expansion, the more cell rupturing, and the soggier the defrosted product. If you freeze fruits, which are high in water, it's okay to serve them while still partially frozen: then you won't notice the degradation that may have occurred in the flesh while it was freezing.

SOMETIMES THE FLAVOR OF SPICES, HERBS, AND SEASONINGS IS ALTERED AS A RESULT OF FREEZING. Spices, like black pepper, and garlic can become bitter when frozen. Salt can just dumb down and lose its oomph. During the testing stage of this book I noticed that the frozen goods in these recipes needed additional salt when used in a dish, although the garlic issue was not a problem. In response, I have refrained from using salt or pepper in the base recipes (although I do use garlic). I had to reject one recipe set that called for ground pork with white wine and thyme, because no matter what I did, the thyme flavor just disappeared; dried thyme does not like to be frozen.

WHAT MAKES FREEZING SAFE?

Freezing inhibits the growth of spoilers that may be on the food. It does not kill them. Keep in mind that you can eat these microbes safely—you do so all the time. You just cannot eat them once they have bloomed, and, in the case of *Clostridium botulinum,* the bacterium that causes botulism, produced toxins. That takes warmth and time and moisture and, in the case of *Clostridium botulinum,* an airless environment. Spoilers cannot bloom at freezing temperatures. They can bloom at room temperatures, and, eventually, some (like molds) can bloom at refrigerated temperatures.

FOODS FREEZE BEST WHEN THEY ARE PRECOOKED. Enzymes, the proteins present in plants and animals that help them mature, are slowed down by freezing. However, if you freeze uncooked foods, the enzymes will continue to age the product—albeit slowly—and undermine the flavor, texture, and color of the food. If the product is cooked before freezing, those enzymes are rendered inactive. Once the recipe has been prepared, allow the food to cool in the refrigerator and then transfer it to the freezer.

There are three options, and you should choose the one best suited to your freezer. Resealable freezer bags are great for recipes like grated apples. They are available at the supermarket, it's easy to press air out of them, and you can lay them flat for storing. Just be sure you use freezer bags and not another kind (it will say on the box), because freezer bags are moisture/vapor proof. This is important, because if the food inside the bag dries out too much, you'll get freezer burn (see below). For purees I use freezer containers. Rubbermaid and Tupperware make them, as do many other companies like Ball and Kerr (which also make canning jars), and you can find them at the grocery store and big-box stores like Kmart. I have used glass jars as well, in which case you must buy jars made for freezing, called "can and freeze," not regular canning jars, which are called "standard." There are lots of websites from which to buy can-and-freeze jars. Lately I have been using freundcontainer.com. Wide-mouthed jars are best (indeed, I prefer them for all my canning, simply because it is easier to get foods in and out of them). I like to use jars because, to a certain extent, you can monitor the foods inside. However, they eat up a lot of real estate in the freezer.

WHAT KIND OF CONTAINERS DO I USE?

The faster the freezing process, the smaller the ice crystals will be and the less damage done to the food's cells. If you cool the food before freezing, it will freeze faster and more evenly.

HOW DO I PACK FOODS TO BE FROZEN?

If you have a separate thermometer in your freezer and can adjust it, turn the freezer down to 0°F or to –10°F. (Lots of spiffy kitchens have Sub-Zero freezers. This is a case where they are very useful.) This will ensure the best freezing conditions. Food stored at 0°F and above will not hold for as long. The storage times noted on these recipes assume your freezer is at 0°F. If it is warmer, then you can't keep the item frozen for as long as I recommend; you won't get sick from it, but the texture won't be as pristine. Indeed, with every 10-degree increase in temperature in your freezer, the foods will decrease in quality, in some cases significantly. *So if you have a warmer freezer, use the foods sooner for best results.* (If you don't have a thermometer, or don't want to bother buying one, just draw some conclusions based on the condition of the other stuff you've got in there: does that bag of frozen blueberries seem less than frozen solid?)

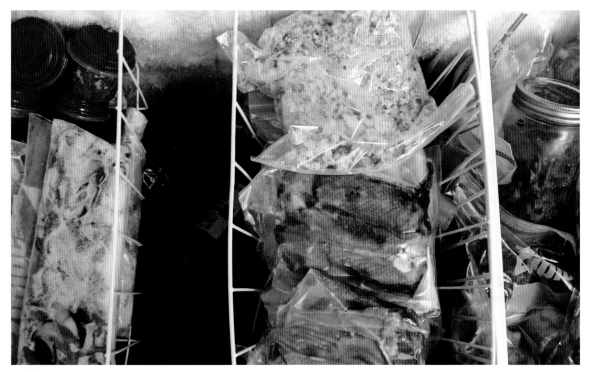

My freezer: mushrooms, bread crumbs, and wild ducks

Fluctuating freezer temperatures can cause some degradation of the quality of your frozen foods as well. If the foods thaw slightly and then refreeze, the tiny, good ice crystals in the cells grow larger and damage the cell walls even more, which undermines the texture of the food. Temperature fluctuations can also cause the water in the foods to migrate out of the tissues, and that leads to drier, tougher foods (this is particularly a problem with frozen meat).

Overpacking the freezer can raise its temperature. To achieve optimum results, you should not try to freeze more than 3 pounds of food per cubic foot of freezer space.

When packing foods in freezer bags, press out as much air as you can, because allowing the surfaces of the food to come into contact with air can eventually cause freezer burn. I have a vacuum-pack machine that my sister gave me, and on the occasions when I have used it, it has worked marvelously well.

When packing foods in jars or plastic containers, be sure to leave about 1 inch of head-space at the top. Because the water in the cells of foods expands when frozen, you'll find your foods will increase slightly in volume. If you don't leave space for this expansion, in the case of plastic containers, the tops will pop off a bit, and your foods will be subjected to greater exposure to the dry environment in the freezer, which leads to freezer burn, or your jars may crack. The environment in your freezer is very dry. That dryness can cause sublimation, the evaporation of water from the tissues of the food and into vapor, if your foods are wrapped improperly. Freezer burn—dried patches on food—won't harm you, but it harms the food's flavor and texture. The foods develop a stale taste and a dry, tough texture in the area of the burn. You can cut freezer burn off the foods it has affected. As long as the rest of the food is free of freezer burn, it will taste okay.

Well, yes. To be honest, I often leave vegetable products on the kitchen counter to thaw out—never meat—but you shouldn't, and I can't recommend it. There are three methods for defrosting foods:

WHAT ABOUT THE WHOLE DEFROSTING-FOODS-IN-THE-FRIDGE THING? DO I HAVE TO DO IT?

1. Thaw them in the refrigerator. This is the safest way, because spoilers won't have a chance to grow during the thawing process. It takes time, but as the recipe volumes are small, you can generally put foods in the refrigerator the night before you plan to use them, even that morning. It is perfectly okay to cook with food that is still crunchy with frost. You can store the defrosted food in the fridge for a couple of days.

2. Thaw in cold water. It's what I end up doing most as I usually forget to pull a product out of the freezer in a timely manner. Fill a large bowl with cold water and place the food in its container in the bowl. The food has to stay in its leakproof container or bag so that bacteria don't slip in via the soaking water and to ensure the food doesn't get waterlogged. Change the water every 30 minutes or so: most of the foods in this book will defrost sufficiently in about 2 hours. You can store the thawed food in the fridge until you are ready to use it (within a couple of days).

3. Thaw in the microwave. You need to cook foods thawed in a microwave right away, as the foods can become warm and even partially cooked in places, which can create an optimal condition for bacteria to grow. Waiting to prepare (i.e., thoroughly heat) a food that has been thawed in a microwave is just not a great idea.

Yes. The only caveat is the frozen food must either be partially frozen or still cold, around 40°F, meaning you defrosted in the fridge *and* the food has been in there for no more than 24 hours. Basically, you can refreeze a previously frozen food if it is in edible condition. Refreezing does undermine the quality of the product, because the already traumatized cells of the food are hit again with expanding ice crystals.

CAN I REFREEZE THAWED FOODS?

PRESERVING IN OIL

I grew up watching my dad slice off blue blooms growing on a hunk of Parmesan cheese before grating it. If a bit of pesto that had peeked above the preserving oil became moldy, he just scooped it off with the tip of a spoon and happily dumped the rest on our pasta. Molds and yeasts, unless they were advanced, were not culinary Cassandras in our house. Rather, they were the small price we paid for the intense flavors of home-preserved goods. Were they inconvenient? Yes. Something you'd like company to see? Only if you wanted to freak them out. But life threatening? It depends on whom you are talking to. My dad is an Italian, and like his mother and grandmother, way back to, I imagine, the seminal Nonna, he preserves a variety of foods in olive oil, as have I, and no one has ever gotten sick.

That said, in 1989 the U.S. Food and Drug Administration warned consumers that there was a risk of botulism food poisoning from some commercial and homemade garlic and oil mixes if left at room temperature instead of refrigerated. *Clostridium botulinum*, the bacterium that causes botulism, is common in nature. But one or more of these conditions—exposure to oxygen, low moisture, acidity, and/or low temperatures—will inhibit the bacterium from producing the botulism toxin. The bacterium is alive but inactive until it gets into a wet, warm, low-acid, airless environment. Then it can, in a matter of 3 or 4 days, produce the toxin that, if ingested, causes paralysis and even death.

If a garlic clove has a few *Clostridium botulinum* spores on it, and you sink that clove into a decanter of oil and leave the decanter at room temperature for a few days, then you have met the requirements for the bacteria to produce the toxin. Lots of people flavor oil with garlic and don't refrigerate it, and very few die. Nonetheless, I don't think you want to be one of those who do. For this reason *you must refrigerate all foods preserved in oil.*

HOW DOES PRESERVING IN OIL WORK?

Preserving in oil is a process whereby foods are protected from airborne spoilers by oil. To preserve in oil, foods that have been heated (like Mushroom Duxelles, page 185) or pickled (like Green Olive Tapenade, page 71) are packed into sterilized jars and covered with olive oil. Good-quality olive oil is in itself airless, as the bits of air trapped in olive oil are centrifugally pressed out during production. Air cannot penetrate olive oil.

Cooking the food (or using acidified foods like olives, which are pickled) before packing it into jars kills most microorganisms on the foods or renders them inert, and the oil acts as a seal between the foodstuff and the environment. Refrigeration ensures *Clostridium botulinum* and other bacteria that may be present remain inert.

If you have concerns, you can always empty a jar of food preserved in oil (or any preserved food) into a pot and boil for 10 minutes (plus 1 minute for each additional 1,000 feet above sea level), and that will destroy any molds, yeasts, or bacteria, including potential botulism toxins that may be present. If the food boils during the course of preparing your recipes, that counts too.

PRESERVING IN A MARINADE MEANS PUTTING UP FOODS IN A COMBINATION OF OIL AND ACID. Spoilers, including *Clostridium botulinum,* are retarded by the acidity in the jar due to the addition of vinegar and/or lemon juice. Preserving in a marinade is similar to pickling, with the addition of olive oil. You can keep marinated foods in the refrigerator for about 10 days, or, if the pH is low enough, you can water bath can marinated foods. Recipes for marinade products that are water bath canned must be calibrated carefully, because (1) the oil-to-vinegar ratio must be such that a pH of 4.5 or less is achieved, and (2) the amount of oil affects how long it takes for heat to penetrate the contents of the jar and bring it up to temperature.

RECIPES FOR PRESERVING IN OIL THAT DO NOT HAVE ENOUGH ADDED ACID TO SUBVERT SPOILERS MUST BE REFRIGERATED. Refrigeration retards the growth of many spoilers, including *Clostridium botulinum.* However, the reason you get mold growing on your Chinese takeout in the fridge is that, while most molds prefer warmer temperatures, some can grow in the cold temperature of your refrigerator. So, how does a food preserved in oil and refrigerated stay mold free? Mold needs 3 things to grow: moisture, food, and air. By covering the foodstuff you have made with oil, you are diminishing the access to air that any lingering molds would need to grow. Foods preserved in oil and refrigerated should be used within 10 days.

It is important to avoid introducing new spoilers into a jar of food preserved in oil. To use less than a full jar of a food that has been preserved in oil and refrigerated, spoon the oil off the top of the jar. Measure out only the amount of food you wish to use. Press the remaining ingredients back down into the jar, re-cover with oil, and return to the refrigerator promptly. Do not allow a whole jar of a food covered with oil to come to room temperature, as that opens the door to the potential development of botulism toxin.

Well, oil. And choosing the right one matters. Mechanically extracted olive oils—usually the most expensive varieties—will stay fluid at lower temperatures than cheaper oils, made by heat or chemical extraction. So a high-quality olive oil is best when preserving foods in oil and then refrigerating. Olive oil will solidify at 42°F, becoming buttery and white.

Oil rancidity is occasionally a problem. The shelf life of oil is about 15 months. Rancid oil has a nasty taste. (One food blogger aptly wrote that it smelled like "old lipstick.") Rancidity is not poisonous, and it's not going to make you sick, nor does it occur in conjunction with the development of botulism toxin or any other spoiler. It happens when polyunsaturated fats (vegetable oil is a polyunsaturated fat) oxidize. Oxidation is a chemical reaction that causes the fats to decompose when exposed to air, sunlight, and heat, in turn producing obnoxious odors and flavors. Refrigeration slows down the march toward rancidity because it is a cool, dark environment, but the oil is still exposed to air (in the bottle) and, of course, time, which stops for no oil.

To prepare marinades, use a vinegar with 5 percent acidity and no sediment. Distilled white vinegar, cider, and wine vinegars are all fine. I don't recommend homemade vinegars due to inconsistency in the amount of acetic acid, although you could test it with a pH meter. I bought mine from the Cole-Parmer Instrument Company (coleparmer.com).

What else do you need? Jars, lids, and bands.

CLEANLINESS IS ALWAYS IMPORTANT. Not fanatical cleanliness, just washing-your-hands-after-riding-the-subway sort of cleanliness. Wash all the ingredients except the dried ones, like nuts and spices, and sterilize the jars you use. To sterilize jars, bring them and their bands to a boil in a large pot of water with a fitted rack. Boil for 10 minutes. Remove the jars with tongs (you don't have to sterilize the tongs). The lids are only simmered in a small pan of hot water, to soften the rubberized flange. (See page 17 for information regarding water bath canning, which applies to the canned marinade recipes in this book.)

THE BASIC TECHNIQUE FOR PREPARING FOODS PRESERVED IN A MARINADE CALLS FOR:

- Partially or completely cooking the foods.
- Boiling the marinade (a combination of vinegar, oil, and flavorings). Overboiling should be avoided, as it can reduce the overall acidity of the marinade.
- Packing the foods into a sterilized jar and covering the foods with the hot marinade. The marinade must totally cover the foods, as the foods will continue to season in the marinade during a short resting period after you have processed the jars in a water bath. Foods that float above the marinade will not season as well. That said, after processing I often see bits of food

sticking up above the marinade. I turn those jars upside down and then back again every few weeks to distribute the marinade more effectively.

- Leaving ½ to ¾ inch of headspace (the space between the top of the marinade and the bottom of the lid). This is important because the heat from the water bath presses the air out of the jar. But if your jar is too full, some of the marinade may be pressed out as well, which could compromise your seal.
- Letting the jars rest in a cool, dark pantry for a few weeks. This will improve the flavor.

THE BASIC TECHNIQUE FOR PREPARING FOODS PRESERVED IN OIL AND REFRIGERATED CALLS FOR:
- Packing the foods in a sterilized jar as tightly as you can, pushing out as much air as you can.
- Wiping the rims of the jars inside and out and totally covering the foods in oil.

Despite my Mediterranean background, I don't preserve in oil without refrigeration or without ensuring the pH level of marinated foods I've water bath canned is 4.5 or lower. However, I don't intend ever to turn down the artichokes my Zia Ada bathes in homemade vinegar, preserves in her cousin's oil, and stores on the shelf. I know. I know. Theoretically I could get sick. Maybe I'll talk it over with Zia at her upcoming birthday party. She'll be ninety.

CURING AND SMOKING

My dad used to cure a ham for prosciutto every winter. The taste was simply wonderful—porky and salty and mild. It was a bit tough though: slicing a piece of it was one of those chores that got bounced among family members until some poor guest or spouse ended up sawing away. But in little chips and bits, the prosciutto lent a terrific blast of flavor to stews and pasta dishes. Dad's prosciutto was also rather brown, the color of liver or an Oxford shoe. That's because he didn't use nitrite in his salt cure, which helps cured meat retain its rich red pigment (as well as effectively inhibiting the growth of harmful bacteria). Nitrite is present in some sea salts, which probably has something to do with the evolution of salt curing. By the same token, the origin of the word *botulism* is *botulus*, Latin for "sausage," suggesting the journey to safe curing, with or without nitrite-laden sea salt, was a long and bumpy road.

My Camerons stovetop smoker secured with wet dish towels (*right*)

Unlike my dad, who has a barn, or my friend Yvon in Colorado, who once tried to cure an elk leg in his garage, I don't have an ideal curing environment. I have a modest-size refrigerator and a hot, sticky New York pad, so refrigerator curing is my only option. But I'm not complaining. I get excellent results curing a few simple products in my apartment.

WHAT IS CURING?

CURING IS THE ART OF PERMEATING FOOD WITH SALT. Salt is sodium chloride. Our bodies need salt to hydrate our cells, as salt helps control the flow of liquid through cell walls. Salt does the same things to the foods we cure: the ions in sodium chloride attract water from cells, and then the salty liquid is reintroduced back into the cells, flowing back and forth through the cell's permeable membrane, seeking a balance of salt in solution.

In large quantities, salt has preservative qualities. Salt urges water from cells, which dehydrates the flesh, and, as spoilers need moisture to grow, salt-cured foods provide an inhospitable environment for microbes. Likewise, salt enters and dehydrates the microbes themselves, further challenging a spoiler's ability to survive.

The surprising thing about salt is that, while it dehydrates cells, the back-and-forth exchange of water and salt through the cell walls actually stretches them out like an old elastic waistband, allowing the cells to hold more moisture (just as a stretched-out waistband allows for a little more of you). That's why you would soak a lean bird like a turkey in saltwater brine before roasting: not for preservation purposes but to create big floppy cells that can hold more moisture, which in turn produces moist, salt-seasoned meat.

TWO STYLES OF CURING: DRY SALTING AND BRINING

DRY SALTING uses salt; sometimes sugar to counteract the harshness or bitterness of the salt; spices or flavorings; and, in the case of some products like fermented sausage, starter cultures and often curing salt (salt mixed with nitrite or nitrite and nitrate). *When dry salting, you rub the salt mixture on the food and chill for a prescribed amount of time.* Then, for the recipes in this book, you remove the salt mixture, allow the food to rest so that the salt distributes itself equally throughout the flesh, and either refrigerate the food (as for Gravlax, page 211), or smoke or otherwise cook the product and then refrigerate it (as for Bacon, page 193).

BRINING could be called *wet salting*. It's also sometimes referred to as a *pickle*. A brine is a mixture of salt and water, sometimes sugar, flavorings, and curing salts, that is heated briefly to dissolve the salt, then chilled, or simply stirred until the salt and sugar dissolve. The food is soaked in this solution for a given amount of time, generally less than needed for a dry salt cure, as dry cures penetrate meat more slowly. After resting in the brine, the food is removed, washed, and either rested or soaked in water to distribute the salt throughout, and usually smoked or otherwise cooked and refrigerated (like Smoked Chicken Breasts, page 198).

WHETHER YOU USE THE DRY SALT OR BRINE METHOD TO CURE FOOD, OF KEY IMPORTANCE IS THE AMOUNT OF SALT YOU APPLY. Regarding the salt content, in general the salt in brines should be 3 percent to 5 percent of the water weight. Water weight is based on how much water it takes to cover the meat by about 3 inches of water, plus the water weight in the food, which is approximately 65 percent of the meat's weight. For a dry cure you use salt weighing 3 percent to 5 percent of the food's weight. In both cases, you use sugar, brown or white, that weighs out at about half of what the salt weighs.

} HOW MUCH SALT DO I USE?

HOW LONG YOU CURE IS BASED ON THE THICKNESS OF THE PRODUCT. For a successful cure, the food must be thoroughly penetrated by salt. So you can expect a 2-pound slab of pork belly to take less time to cure than a 30-pound pork leg. For timing advice for brining chicken you intend to smoke afterward, I turned to the Colorado State University Extension office, where I

} HOW LONG DO I CURE?

took my Master Canner's class. They recommend a brine composed of 1 pound of salt to 1½ gallons of water and a 24-hour brining period for every ½ inch of thickness of the meat.

THE RECIPE FOR BRINING FISH DIFFERS SLIGHTLY. It comes from the Pacific Northwest Extension office, via Kenneth S. Huderbrand, Jr., who is a seafood technologist emeritus at Oregon State University. His advice is to brine fish prior to smoking in a brine that is 1 part salt to 7 parts water. He recommends brining for 30 minutes for a fillet and 2 hours for large hunks of fish. (As a rule, if you use lower-salt solutions, you need to increase the time the food soaks in the brine. Of course, the longer a food is in the brine, the greater the chance bacteria will grow and eventually cause the food to spoil.)

Brine in nonreactive crocks and pans (glass and ceramic are best) and store finished cured products in food-grade resealable plastic bags in the refrigerator or freezer.

ABOUT NITRATE AND NITRITE: I don't use nitrate and nitrite (either potassium or a sodium salt) in my recipes. However, to understand why the bacon made from this book looks different from supermarket bacon, you have to understand the role of these chemicals. Nitrate occurs naturally in water, plants, and earth. When introduced into meats, it encourages the production of nitrite, which has preservative qualities—it is particularly effective against the bacterium that causes botulism—as well as enhancing the flavor and color of meat. A meat cured without nitrite will be grayer than one cured with it. Since the bacon recipe in this book does not call for nitrite, the shelf life and color of the bacon are somewhat compromised. But the method is simple and worry-free, the taste is excellent, and the quantity of bacon produced is small enough to be eaten relatively quickly. I am satisfied with the trade-off.

AN IMPORTANT FACTOR IN THE CURING RECIPES IN THIS BOOK IS "CLEARING," or removing the cure and allowing the salt to complete the task of distributing equally throughout the food. Because the greatest concentration of salt is on the surface of the food, it needs to have the opportunity to complete its penetration into the meat: salt will seek equilibrium throughout all the cells given the time to do so. As for curing, the larger and thicker the food product, the longer it will generally take to clear.

In the case of dry salting, you must clean off the cure thoroughly and allow the meat to rest in the refrigerator for a few hours to allow the salt to disperse evenly. In the case of brining, you must soak the food in clean cold water for a few hours, which accomplishes the same thing.

If you don't clear the food, it will taste very salty. You can use it anyway, but not in a salad, for example. Better to cook it with other foods and add no salt to the dish.

WHAT KIND OF SALT TO USE? Pickling and curing salt and kosher salt are best, as they have no additives or anticaking elements as does iodized salt. Since you don't really know what other minerals might be in sea salts besides sodium and chloride, and as the weight-to-volume ratio of different sea salts varies, you should avoid them for this job.

USE FRESH, GOOD-QUALITY FISH AND MEAT. I've said it before, and I'll say it again: start with an inferior product and you will end with an inferior product. In general, I prefer organic or all-natural meats and wild fish, with the exception of organic Scottish farmed salmon, which is quite fatty and I think makes a more luscious gravlax.

KEEP CURING FOOD CHILLED, BUT NOT SUPER-COLD (below 36°F) or the cure will penetrate the meat too slowly. A consistent temperature of 37°F to 38°F is perfect for achieving a successful cure. The higher the temperature in your refrigerator, the greater the chances are your meat will spoil. (One way you can tell your food is spoiling is a rancid, off odor and a slimy surface on a dry cure and a gunky, thick quality to the brine.)

Once cured, store the food in the fridge or freeze.

SMOKING, a common part two of the curing process, adds incredibly delicious flavor, kills microorganisms through heat, and extends the life of the product.

WHAT IS SMOKING?

TO PREPARE FOR SMOKING, THE CURED FOOD MUST BE DRY. Smoke doesn't adhere to or distribute well on wet surfaces.

ABOUT THE EQUIPMENT: If you live in the suburbs or country, you can use an outdoor smoker—the Indian Chief brand is good and reasonably priced. However, in my New York kitchen, I use a Camerons stovetop smoker, a $48 deal that does the job but leaks like crazy. The manufacturers say I just have to do "the Tweak" to ensure the metal lid fits snugly with no spaces where the smoke can creep out. Tweak? I don't think so. I struggle with the thing every time I smoke and have taken to simply wrapping a few wet dish towels around the rims to keep the smoke in. It's a bit of a hassle, but my recipes don't call for long smoking, and the end product tastes so fabulous I put up with it.

It is best if you have a window or range hood in your kitchen. In my smokiest experiments, I have used a fan to blow excess smoke out my window. It hasn't been a problem with neighbors because the smell of smoked food is not like the smell of smoke from a fire. Smoked food smells delicious. That said, maybe your smoke alarm can't tell the difference.

HOW LONG
DO I SMOKE?

SMOKING TIMES, LIKE BRINING AND CLEARING TIMES, ARE BASED ON THE WEIGHT OF THE FOOD. Ideally you want to reach an internal temperature of 160°F for both fish and poultry. My smoker is quite hot—375°F according to the manufacturer—but I err on the side of safety in these recipes and smoke longer than is called for in the guidelines that come with the smoker, partly because some smoke does escape my smoker and thus lowers the temperature inside.

If your smoker does not get hot enough, the food simply won't cook. I once tried to smoke on a hot plate that I'd rigged up near a window for ventilation purposes, but the coil did not generate enough heat to do the job. Placing the smoker on one gas burner at medium-high does it. So does placing the smoker on my ceramic-top range.

THE MANUFACTURER OF YOUR SMOKER USUALLY SUPPLIES WOOD CHIPS. These are finely ground hardwood chips, like maple, oak, alder, hickory, and fruitwoods. Don't use conifer chips or needles: they leave a nasty taste on the food.

WHEN YOUR SMOKED FOODS ARE COOL ENOUGH TO HANDLE, DRY THEM VERY WELL before you place them in a plastic bag or container and refrigerate or freeze in a freezer bag. Smoked food can sweat, and the moisture released by the food condenses on the inside of the bag and, when it settles on the surface of the food, can create a moist spot where mold can grow. I like to make a nest of paper towels in a plastic container for scallops and wrap chicken breasts in paper towels before refrigeration. It's a bummer to go through the trouble of preserving and then have the food get moldy. I should know. One year my dad gave me a home-cured lonza (the tenderloin of the pig) for Christmas. I ate it enthusiastically for about a week, chucking it into the fridge semiwrapped, where it rubbed up against wet celery and God knows what else, and then I finally wrapped it up in plastic for another two weeks. When I rediscovered it, I tried to wipe off the mold with a dish towel, but it had penetrated too deeply for me to feel comfortable about eating the meat. It was a simple mistake, but it cost me a lonza.

FRUITS

CHERRIES IN WINE

You know summer has finally arrived when the cherries start to come in. The season is short, so in the months that follow I am always grateful that I have taken the time to put some up. These preserves are great used in both savory and sweet dishes. I love having them on hand for unexpected company. All I have to do is dump ½ cup into a wineglass and top with whipped cream for a surprisingly elegant dessert. Cherries have high acidity, as do wine and orange juice, making this a safe product for water bath processing. (See page 17 for information on water bath processing.) I use an olive pitter to pit the cherries.

MAKES 4 PINTS

6 cups red wine

2 cups sugar

2 cups orange juice

24 whole cloves

Sixteen 3-inch strips orange zest

4 pounds Bing cherries, pitted (about 8 cups)

Place the wine, sugar, orange juice, cloves, and orange zest in a medium pot. Bring to a low boil over medium heat, stirring all the while to dissolve the sugar and ensure it doesn't burn.

Have ready 4 scalded pint jars and their bands. (To scald, simply dip the jars in boiling water. You don't need to sterilize the jars, as you will be processing them for over 10 minutes.) Simmer new lids in a small pan of hot water to soften the rubberized flange.

Add the cherries to the wine and simmer for 10 minutes, until they are soft but not collapsed looking. Remove the cherries with a slotted spoon and ladle them into the hot jars.

Reduce the wine mixture remaining in the pot over medium-low heat to about half its volume, about 10 minutes. It will be rather viscous. Strain the wine mixture and pour over the cherries in the jars, leaving ½ to ¾ inch of headspace.

Wipe the rims, set on the lids, and screw on the bands fingertip tight. Place the jars in a big pot with a rack in the bottom and add enough water to cover the jars by 3 inches. Bring to a boil over high heat, then lower the heat to medium and gently boil the jars for 20 minutes. Turn off the heat, allow the jars to rest in the water for 5 minutes, and then remove. Allow the jars to cool, untouched, for 4 to 6 hours. Check the seals and store in a cool, dry place for up to a year. Refrigerate after opening.

CHERRY TENDERLOIN

My friend Mary Dillinger and her boyfriend of twenty-six years, Mark Dorset, came up with the title for this recipe. They thought it sounded like a porn star's name.

In this dish I like the cherries whole. However, you can puree the sauce and then push it through a China cap or fine sieve for a very smooth result. This dish has a kind of Eastern European flavor— it's a tasty way to handle the otherwise mild tenderloin.

2 pounds beef tenderloin, in 4 pieces

1 tablespoon olive oil

1 tablespoon minced garlic

Salt and freshly ground black pepper

1½ cups Cherries in Wine

2 tablespoons unsalted butter

SERVES 4

Preheat the oven to 450°F.

Place the tenderloin pieces on a small broiling pan and bake for 5 minutes. Remove promptly. The meat will look rather gray. It's okay.

Heat the oil in a medium skillet over high heat (do not use a nonstick skillet or you will not have caramelized bits to add flavor to the sauce). Add the tenderloin pieces and sear on one side for 2 minutes. Add the garlic, flip the meat over, and sear for another 2 minutes for medium-rare. Salt the meat. Transfer the meat to a platter, cover, and allow it to rest while you finish the sauce.

Dump the cherries (about 1 cup of fruit) and wine (about ½ cup wine) into the skillet. With a wooden spoon, loosen the garlic bits and caramelized bits of meat stuck to the skillet. Add the accumulated juices from the platter. Simmer for about 4 minutes, then swirl in the butter and simmer 2 minutes more.

Serve the tenderloin sliced on the bias with the sauce on top. Garnish with freshly ground black pepper.

SEARED DUCK BREAST WITH CHERRIES

This is a classic combination. Unlike the tenderloin recipe, here the cherries are pureed, as I find a very refined, smooth sauce better complements the duck breast. I prefer the smaller Long Island duck breasts (descendants of the Pekin duck) to magret, which is the breast of a Moulard duck.

1½ cups Cherries in Wine

2 tablespoons olive oil

Salt and freshly ground black pepper

2 whole Pekin duck breasts, skin scored in a diamond pattern

Fresh rosemary sprigs for garnish (optional)

SERVES 4

Puree the cherries in wine in a food processor until very fine, then push through a China cap or other fine sieve.

Heat the oil in a large skillet over medium heat (if the heat is too high, the duck skin will burn). Salt and pepper the duck breasts. Sear the breasts skin side down in the oil until the skin is golden brown, thin, and crispy, 5 to 7 minutes. Pour off the fat and flip the breasts over. Cook for another 4 minutes for medium-rare. Transfer the breasts to a plate, cover with tin foil, and let them rest.

Pour off the fat in the skillet and add the pureed cherries and the accumulated juices from the duck into the pan. Heat for about 2 minutes, until hot and bubbling.

Slice the duck breast on the bias and serve on a platter dressed with the cherry sauce. Garnish with rosemary sprigs if you like.

CHERRY DESSERT SOUP WITH MASCARPONE

This dessert, which is inspired by Hungarian fruit soups, is easily made ahead of time. I like to serve it in teacups with a thin, crisp cookie.

1 pint Cherries in Wine

1 cup mascarpone cheese

½ cup sugar

½ teaspoon almond extract, or more to taste

SERVES 4

Puree the cherries in a food processor until very smooth, then pass the cherries through a China cap or a very fine sieve. Place in a bowl and cool in the refrigerator.

Place the mascarpone cheese, sugar, and almond extract in a bowl and whip together until smooth (I do it by hand—it takes just a minute). Chill in the refrigerator.

To serve, pour ½ cup of the cherry puree into a serving cup. Garnish with a dollop of almond mascarpone.

APRICOT AMARETTO JAM

Of all the fruit jams and marmalades I make, this one is particularly versatile, I suppose because the apricot taste crosses the sweet and savory line with such finesse. It is equally good mixed into barbecue sauce or combined with whipped cream to make a fool. I have to confess I also prefer this jam because it is so easy to prepare the fruit: just split the apricots in half with a knife and flip out the pits. You don't have to peel them, as the skins are tasty and delicate.

Apricots, which are available in July and August, are high in acidity, making this product safe for water bath processing. Because this recipe calls for a short water bath process, you have to sterilize the jars first. The citric acid will help hold the beautiful orange color of the fruit. The jars will keep in a cool, dark place for up to a year. If, after a few months, you notice the apricots discolor at the top of the jar, don't worry. This happens when excess air gets trapped in the jar, usually because of an air bubble or because there was too much headspace in the jar. If your seals are good, the food is fine. (See page 17 for information on water bath processing.)

MAKES 4 HALF-PINTS

4 cups pitted and chopped apricots
(about ¾ pound)

3 cups sugar

1 tablespoon citric acid (I use Fruit Fresh)

½ teaspoon unsalted butter

3 to 4 tablespoons amaretto

Combine the apricots, sugar, and citric acid in a large, heavy pot and heat over medium-low heat until the sugar melts. Pay attention and stir often, because sugar burns easily. Once the sugar is melted, turn up the heat to medium and bring the apricots to a boil. Add the butter. Apricots tend to foam up as they boil, and if the foam spills over onto your stove you will have quite a mess on your hands. Butter keeps the foam down. Skim off any foam that does form. Cook the apricots, uncovered, at a brisk but not riotous boil. After the first 5 minutes, you will notice that the apricots look thin and soupy. Keep boiling for 15 minutes longer. They will thicken up. You are basically boiling off the water in the fruit. Stir

periodically to make sure the apricots don't stick. Take the apricots off the heat and stir in the amaretto to taste.

Bring 4 half-pint jars and their bands to a boil in a large pot of water fitted with a rack. Boil for 10 minutes. The lids are only simmered in a small pan of hot water, to soften the rubberized flange. Remove the jars with tongs (the tongs don't need to be sterilized). When the jars are dry but still hot, spoon the apricots into the jars with a slotted spoon, leaving 1/2 to 3/4 inch of headspace. (If your apricots were very juicy to start with, you may have extra juice. You can refrigerate it, or boil it down to a thick syrup and can the syrup the same way you do the jam. It is great poured over ice cream and pancakes.) Wipe the rims, set on the lids, and screw on the bands fingertip tight.

Place the jars in a big pot with a rack in the bottom. Add enough water to cover the jars by 3 inches. Bring to a boil over high heat, then lower the heat to medium and gently boil the jars for 10 minutes. Turn off the heat, allow the jars to rest in the water for 5 minutes or so, and then remove. Allow the jars to cool, untouched, for 6 hours. Right away you will hear the popping sound of the vacuum seal as the jars cool down.

Check the seals. Store in a cool, dark place for up to a year. Refrigerate after opening.

Apricot Almond Shortbread

This is a very easy, delicious recipe. Shortbread gets tough when refrigerated for more than 48 hours, and because of the apricots, you do need to refrigerate these squares. So I try not to make more than I plan to eat in a day or so. The recipe doubles easily.

1/3 cup slivered blanched almonds

1 cup all-purpose flour

1/2 cup sugar

8 tablespoons (1 stick) unsalted butter, softened

1/4 cup Apricot Amaretto Jam

MAKES FOUR 4-INCH-SQUARE BARS
Preheat the oven to 375°F. Lightly grease an 8-inch square baking pan.

Pour the almonds onto a baking sheet and place it on the center rack in the oven. Bake the almonds for about 5 minutes, until they are golden and fragrant. Transfer to a bowl and set aside.

In a food processor, pulse to combine the flour, sugar, and butter. The texture will be crumbly and soft. Dump the dough into the prepared baking pan. Using your knuckles, press the dough evenly across the bottom of the pan and create a low edge.

Using the back of a spoon, spread the jam evenly over the dough. Sprinkle the almonds evenly on top.

Bake for 20 minutes, until the edges of the dough are golden brown and the apricots look thickened and glistening. Allow the squares to rest in the oven with the door open for about 5 minutes (the apricots may still be bubbling). Remove the shortbread from the oven and cool in the pan on a rack. When the shortbread is cool, carefully remove the entire shortbread from the pan using a large spatula.

Carefully cut into 4 squares with a sharp knife. (You can also cut the shortbread when it is cool but still in the pan, but that may lead to crumbling.)

Wrap the squares in plastic wrap and refrigerate. They keep for 2 days.

Pork Roast with Apricot Jam and Thyme

Pork is a sweet-tasting meat and, as such, loves to be cooked with fruit. This recipe is adapted from Craig Claiborne's Pork with Garlic. The leftovers, if there are any, make a delicious sandwich, no mayonnaise necessary—just some greens on a whole wheat roll.

1½ pounds pork tenderloin

Salt and freshly ground black pepper

3 garlic cloves, slivered

1 tablespoon olive oil

2 teaspoons dried thyme

1 cup dry white wine

¼ cup Apricot Amaretto Jam

1 cup homemade or all-natural low-sodium chicken stock, or a little more if desired

1 tablespoon unsalted butter (optional)

SERVES 4

Preheat the oven to 350°F.

Season the pork with salt and pepper to taste. Make small slits in the meat with the tip of a sharp knife and insert the garlic slivers. Dribble the meat with olive oil and sprinkle with thyme. Place the meat on a rack in a roasting pan. Pour the white wine into the pan. Roast the meat on the middle rack of the oven for 50 minutes.

Remove the meat from the oven and cut 4 slits in the top. Spoon the jam into the slits and over the meat. Add the stock to the pan and return the roast to the oven for 15 minutes, until the meat is very yielding when prodded with the tines of a fork and pale when you peek into the slits you cut.

Allow the meat to rest for 5 minutes before serving. The drippings are excellent without further preparation—there is very little fat on pork tenderloin. If the browned bits at the bottom of the pan are stuck to the sides, you can add a little more stock and loosen them up with a wooden spoon, then swirl in a tablespoon of butter if you like.

Ricotta Balls Stuffed with Apricot Amaretto Jam

I often simply heat the apricot jam and serve a puddle of it under a couple of ricotta balls for dessert, but stuffing the balls with the jam makes them way more fun to eat—like jelly doughnuts. You will need a pastry decorating bag and a nozzle with a small aperture. The batter can rest for a few hours, but once you fry the ricotta balls they are best stuffed and eaten while still warm. Use fresh or hand-packed ricotta if it is available. Of the commercial brands of ricotta, I prefer Old Chatham Sheepherding Company. Made with sheep and cow's milk, it's the lightest.

1 pound ricotta

3 large eggs, beaten

1 cup all-purpose flour

4 teaspoons baking powder

2 teaspoons grated lemon zest

5 tablespoons amaretto or brandy

Vegetable oil (not olive oil) for frying

½ cup Apricot Amaretto Jam

Confectioners' sugar for garnish

MAKES 16 BALLS

Combine the ricotta, eggs, flour, baking powder, lemon zest, and amaretto in a large bowl. Mix well and refrigerate for about 1 hour.

Heat about 1 inch of oil in a large nonstick skillet over medium-high heat. Test the oil by dropping in a minuscule amount of batter. If the oil boils, it is ready. (You don't want that oil smoking hot, or it will burn your ricotta balls—nor do you want the oil too cool, or the balls will absorb oil and be greasy. After making a ball or two you'll be able to navigate the perfect temperature.)

Have ready a basket lined with paper towels. Drop rounded tablespoons of the batter into the hot oil. Ricotta balls turn golden quickly, but that doesn't mean they are done inside. Cook the balls for 30 seconds or more past the time they look done. (Some cooks like the interior of ricotta balls molten—but not for this recipe.) Drain the balls on the paper towels.

Fit the pastry bag with a plain round lip and attach the coupling ring. Fill the bag with the jam. While the ricotta balls are still warm, stick the tip into the center of a ricotta ball and squeeze in about a teaspoon of the jam. Repeat with the remaining ricotta balls.

Garnish with a sifting of confectioners' sugar and serve warm.

FIGS IN BRANDY

It took having my first child, Carson, for me to appreciate just how much damned time and work my mother had invested in raising me. So in a show of empathy and gratitude, every year for years I gave her a flat of figs, her favorite fruit, on my birthday in the fall. Somehow, her love of figs was transferred to me, and now I can't wait for them to come in. I love to eat fresh figs in pressed focaccia sandwiches with prosciutto or after dinner, with nuts and Gorgonzola cheese. For postseason garnishes and snacking, I put up fresh figs in a light simple syrup.

When it comes to cooking with heat, I prefer to use the more durable dried figs that have been rehydrated in sugar syrup and brandy. These are deliciously sweet and boozy—pureed and spread over shortbread, they make a grown-up Fig Newton (see Apricot Almond Shortbread, page 55; simply replace the apricot jam with pureed figs in brandy). Chopped and stuffed into a baked apple, and served with a shot of thick eggnog, they make a great holiday dessert. But I like them best in savory recipes. Besides the recipes that follow, I like to mix the figs into mashed sweet potatoes.

This recipe is adapted from two sources: the Michigan State University Extension and the *Ball Complete Book of Home Preserving*. The acidity of figs, like that of tomatoes, is borderline, so you must add citric acid (which increases the acidity) to water bath can them safely. The brandy is acidic as well. Allow the figs to season for 2 weeks. Thereafter, they will keep for up to a year. (See page 17 for information on water bath canning.)

MAKES 4 PINTS

2 pounds dried figs (I use Calimyrna), soaked in water to cover in the fridge for 12 hours

1⅓ cups sugar

1¼ cups brandy, plus more for topping off

1 teaspoon citric acid (I use Fruit Fresh)

Drain the soaked figs and place them in a large pot with 6 cups of water. Bring to a boil over medium-high heat and boil, uncovered, for 15 minutes. Add the sugar and allow the figs to return to a boil. Boil rapidly for about 2 minutes until the sugar is dissolved and then stir in 1 cup of the brandy.

Have ready 4 scalded pint jars and their bands. (To scald, simply dip the jars in boiling water. You don't need to sterilize the jars, as you will be

< DUCK BREAST WITH BRANDIED FIG SAUCE

processing them for over 10 minutes.) Simmer new lids in a small pan of hot water to soften the rubberized flange. In the bottom of each jar, place ¼ teaspoon citric acid. Stuff in the figs and cover them with the brandy syrup, leaving ½ to ¾ inch of headspace. If there is not enough brandy syrup, bring the liquid up to within 1 inch of the rim with extra brandy. Wipe the rims, set on the lids, and screw on the bands fingertip tight.

Place the jars on a rack in a big pot and add enough water to cover the jars by 3 inches. Cover the pot and bring to a boil over high heat, then lower the heat to medium and boil the jars gently for 20 minutes. Turn off the heat, remove the cover, and then, after about 5 minutes, remove the jars from the water bath. Allow the jars to cool, untouched, for 4 to 6 hours. Check the seals and store in a cool, dark place for up to a year, allowing them to season for 2 weeks before using them. They'll continue to season over the course of the year, developing a more mellow taste. Refrigerate after opening.

DUCK BREAST WITH BRANDIED FIG SAUCE

You can use either 2 whole Pekin breasts or 1 whole magret breast in this recipe—magret takes a bit longer to cook. Be sure to cut most of the fat off the magret breast before cooking, or you risk overcooking the duck before the fat has rendered enough. Don't throw away that fat, though! Render it and store in a food-grade container in the fridge for up to a year (it also freezes). It is a delicious, healthy cooking fat.

¼ cup olive oil

2 tablespoons chopped fresh sage or 1 tablespoon dried

2 garlic cloves, minced (about 1 tablespoon)

1 teaspoon grated orange zest

Pinch of hot red pepper flakes

Salt

2 whole Pekin duck breasts or 1 whole magret, split, with all but ¼ inch of fat removed

2 tablespoons minced shallot

1 pint Figs in Brandy, figs coarsely chopped, syrup reserved

1 cup homemade or all-natural low-sodium chicken stock

2 tablespoons unsalted butter

2 tablespoons minced fresh flat-leaf parsley, and/or 1 teaspoon grated orange zest for garnish

SERVES 4

In a large bowl, stir together the oil, sage, garlic, orange zest, hot red pepper flakes, and salt to taste. Add the duck breasts and flip them over in the marinade a few times to coat. Cover and place in the refrigerator for about 30 minutes.

Heat a large skillet over medium heat. Carefully add the duck breasts fat side down. Brown the breasts, 5 to 7 minutes on the fat side, 4 minutes on the other side. Duck breasts are tastiest and most tender served medium-rare. Remove the breasts; place them on a platter and cover with foil.

If there is more than 2 tablespoons of fat in the skillet, pour off the excess. Add the shallot and cook over medium-low heat until translucent, a few minutes. Add the chopped figs and syrup to the skillet, then stir in the stock. Turn the heat up to medium-high and boil gently, stirring to loosen the browned bits, for about 5 minutes, until the sauce is reduced by half. Swirl in the butter and cook until it melts. Adjust the seasoning.

Slice the duck breasts on the bias.

Pour any duck juices that have accumulated on the platter into the sauce and continue cooking the sauce for a few minutes to meld the flavors.

Pour most of the sauce onto a serving platter and arrange the sliced duck breasts on top. Dribble additional sauce over the duck meat. Serve garnished with parsley, orange zest, or both.

CHICKEN AND BRANDIED FIG ROLLATINI

These elegant little rolls of delicate chicken cutlet stuffed with brandy-infused figs balance savory and sweet flavors surprisingly well. I tie them up like miniroasts—the most time-consuming part of this recipe—and they look beautiful on the plate, especially when resting on a bed of sautéed spinach or escarole.

8 chicken scaloppine

Salt and freshly ground black pepper

1 pint Figs in Brandy

2 tablespoons olive oil

1 cup dry white wine

½ cup homemade or all-natural low-sodium chicken stock if needed

SERVES 4

Preheat the oven to 375°F.

Season the cutlets with salt and pepper to taste. Drain the figs, reserving the syrup. Cut the figs into bite-sized pieces. Place about 2 tablespoons of fig on each cutlet and roll it up, tucking in the ends. With cooking twine, tie up the rolls as you would a roast.

Heat the oil in a medium skillet over medium-high heat. Add the rollatini and brown them all over, about 5 minutes. Place the rollatini in a baking pan. Add the white wine and the fig syrup. Bake, covered with tin foil, for 30 minutes, until the chicken is cooked through but very tender. If the pan seems dry at any point, add the chicken stock.

To serve the rollatini, cut the strings and discard. Dribble the drippings over the rollatini.

VEAL BREAST WITH BRANDIED FIGS

Every spring I make veal breast once or twice. A whole veal breast makes a marvelous party dish because it is served at room temperature and looks gorgeous on the plate. The meat is tender and pink, and the ricotta/fig stuffing, which is bound with egg, is flavorful and rich. This is an adaptation of my dad's recipe.

Veal breast is getting easier to find at the markets. You want a thin, flat piece of meat that is generally rectangular, as you will be rolling and tying it up. The breast must be tied, especially at the ends, as the ricotta becomes loose when it heats up and can leak out. You can also wrap the breast in cheesecloth before baking. The instructions for both procedures follow.

One 2-pound piece boned veal breast, fat trimmed, cut into a rectangle

Salt and freshly ground black pepper

½ cup ricotta

½ cup Figs in Brandy, drained and finely chopped

1 large egg, beaten

Pinch of freshly grated nutmeg

1 tablespoon olive oil

1 teaspoon dried rosemary or 1 tablespoon chopped fresh

1 cup Marsala wine

SERVES 4

Preheat the oven to 450°F.

Season the veal breast with salt and pepper to taste.

Mix together the ricotta, figs, egg, nutmeg, and salt and pepper to taste in a small bowl. Blend well. Lay the veal flat and spread the surface with the stuffing. Be careful not to place the stuffing too close to the edges of the meat. Gently roll the veal as you would a jelly roll. Tie with string, being sure the ends are closed up well. For best results, sew up the ends with a trussing needle. Rub the roll with the oil and sprinkle with rosemary.

As an alternative, you can wrap the entire roll in cheesecloth before tying. The cheesecloth will hold the stuffing in. If you use cheesecloth, add the olive oil and rosemary before wrapping up the roll.

Gently place the roll in a baking pan just large enough to hold the veal, seam side down. Roast, uncovered, for 40 minutes, until the meat is browned. Add the Marsala to the pan, basting the veal well, and cover the veal with foil. Continue cooking for 20 minutes, basting once or twice.

Remove the meat and let it rest on a platter for about 3 hours, until it is at room temperature. Cut into slices and serve or refrigerate. The veal is excellent the next day.

CONCORD GRAPE WALNUT CONSERVE

Conserves, which combine fruit and nuts, are traditionally served as a condiment with a meal or in desserts. This conserve, made with the foxy-tasting Concord grape (in season in the fall), is not overly sweet and marries very well with chocolate and pastry of all sorts. It's also good served on a cheese platter. This recipe is adapted from *So Easy to Preserve* from the University of Georgia Cooperative Extension. Grapes and oranges are both high in acidity, and since spoilers cannot thrive in the moistureless environment of dried nuts, this product is safe for water bath processing. (See page 17 for information on water bath canning.) The conserve keeps for up to a year.

MAKES 6 HALF-PINTS

8 cups stemmed Concord grapes
(about 4 pounds), preferably seedless

6 cups sugar

Six 2-inch-long strips orange zest

2 cups walnuts, semicrushed

Place the grapes, sugar, and ½ cup of water in a heavy pot over medium heat. Mash the grapes with a potato masher as they heat up. Stir frequently to ensure the sugar dissolves without burning. Cook for 10 to 20 minutes, until the grapes are tender; remove them from the heat. As soon as they are cool enough to handle, push the grapes through a food mill to separate out the skins and seeds. You will have a thick juice. Return to the pot. Add the orange zest and boil gently for 15 to 20 minutes over medium heat, until the mixture thickens. Keep an eye on it: the mixture can foam up and spill over the edge of the pot. Add the walnuts and continue cooking for 5 minutes.

Have ready 6 scalded half-pint jars and their bands. (To scald, simply dip the jars in boiling water. You don't need to sterilize the jars, as you will be processing them for over 10 minutes.) Simmer new lids in a small pan of hot water to soften the rubberized flange. Pour the conserve into the jars leaving ½ to ¾ inch of headspace; wipe the rims, set on the lids, and screw on the bands fingertip tight.

Place the jars in a big pot with a rack in the bottom and add enough water to cover the jars by 3 inches. Bring to a boil over high heat, then boil the jars for 30 minutes. Turn off the heat, allow the jars to rest in the water for 5 minutes or so, and then remove. Allow the jars to cool, untouched, for 4 to 6 hours. Right away you will hear the popping sound of the vacuum seal as the jars cool down. If the walnuts are floating when you remove them from the water bath, it's okay. Just cool the jars upside down.

Check the seals. Store in a cool, dark place for up to a year. Refrigerate after opening.

BAKED BRIE WITH CONCORD GRAPE WALNUT CONSERVE

Baked Brie is a reliable if unexciting holiday standby. However, the addition of Concord grape and walnut conserve really wakes this dish up. You can substitute Camembert for Brie, but it is a little stronger tasting. (For that matter, you can substitute Apricot Amaretto Jam, page 53, and sliced blanched almonds for the conserve.) I use Dufour frozen puff pastry, which is available at most gourmet shops. You can call 800-439-1282 for retailers that carry it.

1 small round Brie cheese (750 grams), chilled

3 tablespoons Concord Grape Walnut Conserve

7 ounces frozen puff pastry, defrosted

1 large egg yolk, beaten

SERVES 4 AS AN HORS D'OEUVRE

Preheat the oven to 350°F.

Place the well-chilled cheese on a piece of wax paper or plastic wrap. With a long knife, slice the cheese in half horizontally, as you would a roll for a sandwich. Spoon the conserve onto the bottom half of the cheese, then replace the top half. Wrap the cheese in the wax paper or plastic and refrigerate while you roll out the pastry.

On a lightly floured board, roll out the pastry about ⅛ inch thick. Place the pastry in a pie pan. Unwrap the Brie and place it in the center of the pastry. Fold the dough over the pastry—do not stretch it or you will create weaknesses in the dough through which the conserve and cheese may seep out. Pinch the dough at the seams to seal. Brush the top of the pastry with the egg yolk. This will make the baked pastry shiny.

Bake the Brie, uncovered, for about 15 minutes, until the pastry is golden.

Allow the baked Brie to rest for a few minutes before serving with French or Italian bread. (A small pie knife is best for service.)

Fried Grape and Walnut Ravioli with Chocolate

This is a variation on a traditional Christmas dessert made in Italy that is composed of wine grape must, walnuts, and chocolate. The easy ravioli is my grandmother's recipe, and it is a great one; you can use it for classic savory ravioli dishes as well. You don't have to use a pasta machine for this dish—my grandmother always rolled it out by hand, using a broomstick—but it makes a much more delicate and tender ravioli if you do.

FOR THE PASTA

1½ cups all-purpose flour

Pinch of salt

2 large eggs

1 half-pint jar Concord Grape Walnut Conserve, orange zest removed

⅓ cup semisweet chocolate grated on the large holes of a box grater

Vegetable oil (not olive oil) for frying

Confectioners' sugar for garnish

SERVES 4

To make the pasta, combine the flour and salt and mound on a board. Make a well in the center of the mound and crack the eggs into the well. Using a fork, gradually combine the flour with the eggs. When half of the flour is incorporated, switch to using your hands. Combine the flour and eggs thoroughly. You may need to add water. Add 1 tablespoon at a time until the dough is soft enough to knead easily. Knead for about 15 minutes, until the pasta is smooth and pliable, and form into a ball. Rub a few drops of olive oil all over the dough, cover it in plastic, and leave it at room temperature for about 1 hour.

Combine the conserve and the chocolate in a small bowl.

Cut the pasta ball in half. Pass each half through the rollers of a pasta machine in ever-decreasing thicknesses, until the pasta has passed through the narrowest width. (If you roll it out by hand, just keep at it: you want the pasta to be as thin as you can get it, about ⅛ inch.) Lay a length of pasta out on a floured board. Place 12 to 16 teaspoon-sized dollops of conserve on the pasta about 3 inches apart. (You can also use a ravioli mold.) Top with the second sheet of pasta. Cut out the ravioli (you can also use a three-inch round cookie cutter). Have ready a small cup of water. Wet the tines of a fork and press firmly all along the edges of the ravioli to seal.

Heat about ¾ inch of vegetable oil in a medium nonstick skillet over medium-high heat until very hot. (You can test the oil by tossing a pinch of flour in. If it boils up furiously, the oil is ready.) Do not let the oil smoke or your ravioli could burn.

Carefully place the ravioli in the hot oil in batches and cook for about 10 seconds on each side, until they are golden brown and puffy. Remove with a slotted spoon and drain on paper towels.

Garnish the ravioli with a dusting of confectioners' sugar.

NOTE Do not serve the ravioli immediately—the jelly inside is hot! Let them rest a few minutes.

CONCORD GRAPE WALNUT TART

This tart is not too sweet, very grapey, with a subtle orange flavor. The leftovers are excellent with coffee as a morning pastry. You can add about 1/4 cup semisweet chocolate grated on the big holes of a box grater to this tart if you like.

1¼ cups all-purpose flour

¼ cup confectioners' sugar

4 tablespoons (½ stick) unsalted butter, cut up

1 large egg

1 teaspoon grated orange zest

¼ teaspoon salt

2 half-pint jars Concord Grape Walnut Conserve, orange zest removed

About 20 fresh globe grapes, peeled, halved, and seeded (see Note)

1 cup heavy cream

3 tablespoons granulated sugar

3 tablespoons Marsala wine

MAKES ONE 9-INCH TART

To make the pastry, place the flour, confectioners' sugar, butter, egg, orange zest, and salt in a food processor and pulse until the dough comes together. Form the dough into a ball, wrap in wax paper, and place in the refrigerator to rest for 30 minutes.

Place the oven rack in the lower third of the oven. Preheat the oven to 350°F.

Place the rested dough on a lightly floured surface and pat it in all directions with a floured rolling pin. Roll the dough from the center out to a thickness of about 1/8 inch, loosening the pastry from the surface and reflouring the rolling pin and surface as necessary. Fold the pastry gently into quarters or roll it up on the rolling pin and transfer it to a buttered 9-inch tart pan. (Don't use a removable-bottom tart pan.) Fit the dough into the pan loosely and press it against the pan without stretching it.

Spread the conserve evenly on the pastry. (If you are adding chocolate, stir them together in a small bowl first.) Arrange the grapes in concentric circles over the conserve. Place the tart on a cookie sheet and bake until the pastry crust turns light brown, about 35 minutes. Let the tart sit until it cools completely before serving—up to an hour. While cooking, the conserve will liquefy. As it cools, the conserve will firm up again.

In the meantime, whip the heavy cream in a cold metal bowl until it holds peaks, about 2 minutes with an electric beater, more if you are whisking by hand. Slowly add the granulated sugar in a steady stream as you continue whipping. Gently fold in the Marsala.

Serve the tart with dollops of Marsala cream.

NOTE Instead of topping with the globe grapes, you can roll about a quarter of the dough into six 10-inch-long strips and make a lattice.

GREEN OLIVE TAPENADE

This is a savory condiment that lends a fresh-tasting Mediterranean quality to dishes. You need to add very little to infuse a dish with its flavor. Try a dollop in place of the olives in just about any recipe you have and you will be pleasantly surprised! It is also delicious on bruschetta (small slices of toasted Italian bread), either on its own or combined with sweet butter.

Tapenade is composed primarily of cured and pickled products (olives and capers), which are hostile to spoilers. The tapenade is refrigerated, which retards the growth of any spoilers in the jar, and covered in oil, which acts as a barrier between the food and the air in the fridge and prevents the introduction of new spoilers. (See page 37 for information on preserving in oil.) Covered in oil and refrigerated, the tapenade lasts 10 days.

MAKES 3 HALF-PINTS

1 pound large mild green olives (about 45 olives), such as Cerignola, pitted (see Note)

3 garlic cloves, sliced (about 1½ tablespoons)

2 tablespoons pine nuts

2 tablespoons olive oil, plus oil to cover

1 tablespoon fresh thyme leaves or 1 teaspoon dried

1½ teaspoons drained capers

¼ teaspoon hot paprika

Salt

Place the olives, garlic, pine nuts, 2 tablespoons olive oil, thyme, capers, hot paprika, and salt to taste in a food processor and pulse to grind to a paste.

Bring 3 half-pint jars and their bands to a boil in a large pot of water fitted with a rack. Boil for 10 minutes. Remove the jars with tongs (the tongs don't need to be sterilized). Simmer new lids in a small pan of hot water to soften the rubberized flange. When the jars are dry but still hot, pack in the tapenade, eliminating as many air pockets as you can. (I press down with the knuckles of my index and middle fingers to pack the sauce—be sure your hands are clean.) Fill the jars to about 1 inch below the rim. Add a ½-inch layer of olive oil to cover. Wipe the rim with a damp paper towel, place on the lid, and screw on the band fingertip tight. Refrigerate for 24 hours, then check the tapenade to see if you need to add more olive oil to cover due to absorption.

The tapenade can be stored in the refrigerator for 10 days. Be sure to cover the surface of the tapenade with oil after each use. Remove only the quantity of tapenade that you need for a dish and allow that to come to room temperature. Cover the remaining tapenade in the jar with oil and return it to the fridge promptly.

NOTE To remove olive pits quickly, smash the olive with the flat side of a cook's knife. This cracks the flesh and exposes the pit.

Pizza with Mozzarella and Green Olive Tapenade

I love to serve this pizza as an hors d'oeuvre. Its tangy saltiness is excellent with cocktails (okay—martinis). The dough is adapted from *Cook's Illustrated,* my favorite nerdy food magazine. It's terrific (the magazine and the dough).

FOR THE DOUGH

2 cups unbleached all-purpose flour

½ teaspoon active dry yeast

½ teaspoon sugar

½ teaspoon salt

2 teaspoons olive oil

2 tablespoons fine cornmeal

1 cup mozzarella cheese grated on the large holes of a box grater

⅔ cup Green Olive Tapenade

2 teaspoons olive oil

Salt and freshly ground black pepper

MAKES TWO 10-INCH PIZZAS

Pulse the flour, yeast, sugar, and salt in a food processor to combine. Continue to pulse, adding ½ cup of water, then the oil. The dough will come together, either like a mass of little moist curdles or as a ball. Both are good. (If it does not come together, add 2 to 4 tablespoons water—not all at once, since environmental factors can affect how much water you need.) Dump the dough onto your work surface, press it together, then slap it around on the counter a few times. Knead the dough for about 3 minutes. Place the dough in a resealable plastic bag and refrigerate overnight (2 days is okay).

Preheat the oven to 425°F.

Cut the dough into 2 pieces and knead them a few times to roll each into a tidy ball. I use ceramic pizza stones to make pizza, but you can use cookie sheets too. Place the pizza stones in the oven to preheat. Sprinkle 1 tablespoon of cornmeal onto your work surface. Roll one ball of dough out, flip it over, and roll to a 10-inch diameter. (Or roll it larger

if you can. When the dough retracts a little at the edges when you roll it out, you have rolled it out as far as it can go.) Repeat with the second ball of dough and the second tablespoon of cornmeal. Place the pizzas on the warm pizza stones.

Dribble a teaspoon of olive oil over each pizza and place the pizzas in the hot oven. Cook for about 5 minutes, until the dough begins to puff up and look chalky. Remove the pizzas, stick a few holes in the bubbles with the tines of a fork, and sprinkle on the cheese. Spread the tapenade over the cheese. Add salt and pepper to taste. Return the pizzas to the oven and cook for about 10 minutes, until the edges of the pizzas are golden and the cheese is melted. Serve immediately.

MACKEREL WITH GREEN OLIVE TAPENADE

Any "green," or oily, fish, like butterflied sardines, can be substituted for the mackerel. This is a very elegant dish, wonderful with a green salad.

3 tablespoons olive oil

1½ pounds fresh mackerel fillets (four fillets about 9 inches long), skin on

Salt and freshly ground black pepper

¼ cup Green Olive Tapenade

SERVES 4

Place your oven rack about 6 inches below the broiler. Preheat the broiler.

Pour the oil into a broiler pan and use your fingers to rub the oil all over the surface. Add the fillets and flip them a couple of times to ensure they are coated with oil. Place the fillets in the pan skin side down. Season with salt and pepper to taste.

Place the fish under the broiler for about 5 minutes if you are using an electric broiler, a few minutes less if your oven is gas. The mackerel must be about three-quarters of the way cooked through. (Check it by gently separating the flesh of a fillet with the tines of a fork. The meat should be almost opaque throughout.) Remove the fish and, using a wide flat knife, spread 1 tablespoon of tapenade over each fillet. Return the fish to the broiler and continue to cook for 3 minutes to finish cooking the fish and thoroughly heat the tapenade. Serve immediately.

CHICKEN THIGHS WITH GREEN OLIVE TAPENADE

One of my favorite recipes from Le Marche, the region of Italy that my father comes from, is braised chicken with Ascoli olives—large green olives that have been cured in lime (the mineral, not the fruit). This recipe is an adaptation that I like to serve with rice. We eat it hot out of the pan or at room temperature. Both are good.

8 chicken thighs

3 tablespoons olive oil

4 garlic cloves, minced (about 2 tablespoons)

2 fresh rosemary branches, about 3 inches long (optional)

1 cup dry white wine

6 tablespoons Green Olive Tapenade

SERVES 4

Loosen the meat next to the bone slightly with the tip of a sharp knife. (Loosening the thigh meat next to the bone ensures even cooking.)

Heat the olive oil in a large nonstick skillet or seasoned cast-iron skillet over medium heat. Add the chicken thighs skin side down. Cook for about 15 minutes, until the skin is nicely browned and separates easily from the pan. Flip the thighs over and cook for another 15 minutes. Pour off all but a tablespoon or two of the chicken fat. Leave the chicken thighs in the pan. Add the garlic and rosemary and cook for a couple minutes, until the garlic becomes soft. Add the wine, cover, and boil for about 5 minutes, then remove the cover and let the wine cook down for a few minutes more. Stir in the tapenade and ¼ cup water and cook for 5 minutes, until the sauce is heated through.

PEAR, PORT, AND THYME CONSERVE

This fruit conserve is surprisingly delicate. It is lovely served beside a piece of roasted chicken, duck, or pork. But it also has real heft flavorwise, so it can stand up next to the strong tastes of butternut squash, molasses, and ginger, as the following recipes attest. It is especially good served with additional fresh thyme.

The recipe is adapted from *Ball Complete Book of Home Preserving*. Pears are high in acidity, and as spoilers cannot thrive in the moistureless environment of dried nuts and raisins, this product is safe to water bath process. (See page 17 for information on water bath canning.)

MAKES 5 HALF-PINTS

½ cup golden raisins (brown are okay, too)

½ cup light brown sugar

½ cup fresh-squeezed orange juice

¼ cup bottled lemon juice

1 tablespoon grated lemon zest

½ teaspoon ground cinnamon

½ teaspoon freshly grated nutmeg

½ teaspoon ground ginger

Pinch of salt

3 pounds Bosc or Anjou pears, peeled, cored, and coarsely chopped (about 5 cups)

½ cup sliced blanched almonds

¼ cup port wine

1 tablespoon chopped fresh thyme

Combine the raisins, brown sugar, orange and lemon juices, lemon zest, cinnamon, nutmeg, ginger, and salt in a large pot. Stir to dissolve the sugar. Bring to a boil over medium-high heat. Add the pears, cover, lower the heat, and boil gently for 15 minutes. Remove the cover and cook for another 15 minutes to thicken. Stir in the almonds, port, and thyme.

Have ready 5 scalded half-pint jars and their bands. (To scald, simply dip the jars in boiling water. You don't need to sterilize the jars, as you will be processing them for over 10 minutes.) Simmer new lids in a small pan of hot water to soften the rubber-ized flange. Pour the conserve into the jars, leaving ½ to ¾ inch of headspace; wipe the rims, set on the lids, and screw on the bands fingertip tight.

Place the jars in a big pot with a rack in the bottom and add enough water to cover the jars by

< BUTTERNUT SQUASH SOUP WITH PEAR, PORT, AND THYME CONSERVE

3 inches. Bring to a boil over high heat. Boil the jars for 20 minutes. Turn off the heat, allow the jars to rest in the water for 5 minutes or so, and then remove. Allow the jars to cool, untouched, for 4 to 6 hours.

Check the seals and store in a cool, dark place for up to a year. Refrigerate after opening.

BUTTERNUT SQUASH SOUP WITH PEAR, PORT, AND THYME CONSERVE

This is an adaptation of a squash soup prepared by Leslie Li, the chef at the Rudolf Steiner School in Manhattan—it's a testament to how great institutional food can be. Chef Li uses local, organic fruits and vegetables and prepares the dishes in simple, tasteful ways. The kids love it. So do I.

Squash and pear conserve go very well together, so you can experiment with this great combination. Try roasting the squash and then throwing it in a sauté pan with the conserve and a dab of butter to serve as a side dish. You can also use the squash in a pumpkin pie recipe with ½ cup of conserve added to the filling.

3 pounds butternut squash, peeled, seeded, and cubed

¼ cup olive oil

Salt and freshly ground black pepper

1 medium onion, chopped (about 1 cup)

3 celery stalks, chopped (about 1 cup)

2 teaspoons chili powder

1 tablespoon light brown sugar

1 quart homemade or all-natural low-sodium chicken stock

2 tablespoons unsalted butter

2 half-pint jars Pear, Port, and Thyme Conserve

Fresh thyme for garnish

SERVES 4

Preheat the oven to 400°F.

Toss the cubed squash in a large bowl with 2 tablespoons of the olive oil. Season with salt and pepper to taste and spread on a baking sheet. Place the squash in the oven and roast until very tender when pierced with a fork, about 40 minutes. If the cubes caramelize (brown) a bit around the edges, this is good. Remove from the oven.

Heat the remaining 2 tablespoons of olive oil in a large Dutch oven over medium heat. Add the onion and celery and cook until the onion is translucent, about 5 minutes. Add the chili powder and brown sugar and stir to coat. Add the squash and stock. Bring the stock to a boil, then lower the heat to medium-low and cook for 5 to 10 minutes, until the flavors have melded.

Puree the soup by using an immersion blender or by allowing the stock to cool and then pureeing it in a food processor a cup at a time. You can also press the soup through a food mill.

Return the pureed soup to the heat and add the butter. Stir in the butter while the soup simmers over medium-low heat, until the butter is melted and the soup is hot, a few minutes. Add the conserve, reserving ¼ cup for garnish.

To serve, ladle the soup into bowls and garnish each bowl with 1 tablespoon of the conserve and a sprig of fresh thyme.

VEAL TAILS WITH PEAR, PORT, AND THYME CONSERVE

Veal tails are very delicious, though there isn't much meat on them. They used to be hard to find, but I am finding them more and more often in markets. You can make this dish with oxtails too, which are more readily available. Either way, look for the meatiest cuts. And lay in the bread; this dish is very savory, and you'll want to sop up the sauce.

3 pounds veal tails

Salt and freshly ground black pepper

3 tablespoons olive oil

1 medium onion, chopped (about 1 cup)

4 garlic cloves, sliced (about 2 tablespoons)

½ cup dry white wine

1 tablespoon chopped fresh rosemary or 1 teaspoon dried

¾ pound small potatoes, peeled and quartered (I like to use German Butterball or baby Yukon Gold)

¾ cup homemade or all-natural low-sodium chicken stock

2 tablespoons chopped fresh flat-leaf parsley

1 half-pint jar Pear, Port, and Thyme Conserve

SERVES 4

Season the veal tails with salt and pepper to taste.

Heat the oil in a large skillet over medium-high heat. Add the veal tails and brown, about 3 minutes per side. Turn the heat down to medium and add the onion and garlic. Cook until the onion is translucent, about 5 minutes. Add the wine and rosemary, cover, and cook for 5 minutes. Remove the cover and add the potatoes, stock, and parsley. Cook, covered, for 30 minutes, until the potatoes are soft. Remove the cover and cook for 10 minutes or so, until the sauce thickens. Add the conserve and cook for a few minutes, until the pears are heated through. Adjust the seasoning.

Serve right away or cover and serve later, in which case, you will need to add a little more stock during reheating.

GINGERBREAD WITH PEAR, PORT, AND THYME CONSERVE

This is a very moist, cozy dessert that should be eaten while still warm. If you don't, wrap it well in plastic and refrigerate. Gingerbread is notorious for drying out quickly.

4 tablespoons (½ stick) unsalted butter, softened

½ cup granulated sugar

1 large egg, beaten

1¼ cups all-purpose flour

¾ teaspoon baking soda

1 teaspoon ground ginger

½ teaspoon ground cinnamon

¼ teaspoon salt

½ cup dark molasses

¼ cup hot water

1 half-pint jar Pear, Port, and Thyme Conserve

Confectioners' sugar for garnish

SERVES 4

Place the oven rack in the center of the oven. Preheat the oven to 350°F. Butter a 9 x 5-inch loaf pan.

In a large bowl, beat the butter and sugar together until light. Add the egg and continue beating until it is thoroughly mixed in. In a medium bowl, sift together the flour, baking soda, ginger, cinnamon, and salt. In a small bowl, combine the molasses and hot water.

Add half of the flour mixture to the butter mixture and stir until blended. Add half of the molasses mixture and stir until blended. Add the remaining flour mixture and stir until blended. Add the remaining molasses mixture and stir until blended.

Pour the conserve into the bottom of the pan, distributing it as evenly as possible, then pour the batter over the conserve. Bake the gingerbread for about 40 minutes, until a knife slid into the bread comes out clean. Do not overcook. Allow to cool slightly before turning out onto a rack.

Serve warm, dusted with confectioners' sugar.

PRESERVED MEYER LEMONS

A staple of Moroccan, Algerian, and Tunisian cuisine, preserved lemons are sweetly sour and salty and add a wallop of flavor to any dish that calls for a strong lemon flavor, including condiments like homemade mayonnaise and vinaigrette. However, they are intense and should be used in moderation. There are about a thousand recipes for preserved lemons out there. This one, which I like best of all those I have tried, is a confluence of many. I like the tangeriney quality of Meyer lemons, which are a winter fruit, but you can preserve any kind of lemons with this recipe.

Preserved lemons are a type of pickle made by the dry salt method: brined in salt and the lemon's own juices. Preserved Meyer lemons are very acidic—way too acidic to nurture spoilers. After the curing process, they are stored in the refrigerator. (See page 40 for more information on curing.)

MAKES 2 PINTS

10 Meyer lemons, regular lemons, or a combination (see Note), scrubbed

½ cup kosher salt

With a sharp knife, remove the stem ends of 6 of the lemons. Slice the lemons into quarters from pole to pole.

Bring 2 wide-mouth pint jars and their bands to a boil in a large pot of water fitted with a rack. Boil for 10 minutes. Remove the jars with tongs (the tongs don't need to be sterilized). Simmer new lids in a small pan of hot water to soften the rubberized flange. When the jars are dry but still hot, shove the lemon wedges into the jars, trying not to crush the fruit too much, but do pack them in, sprinkling 3 tablespoons of salt per jar as you go and making sure the salt is well distributed throughout. Meyer lemons are softer than regular lemons and therefore easier to squash down into the jar.

Juice the remaining 4 lemons. Top each jar with 1 final tablespoon of salt, then distribute the juice between the jars, making sure the lemon wedges are completely covered with juice. If you see air bubbles along the side of the jar, slip a butter knife

down into it and press aside the fruit to allow juice to fill the space. You may need more lemon juice depending on the juiciness of your lemons.

Set on the lids, and screw on the bands fingertip tight. Let the lemons ferment on your kitchen counter for 2 weeks for Meyer lemons, 3 to 4 weeks for regular lemons, which have tougher skins, and ferment until they are soft enough to tear. Turn the jars upside down every other day to make sure the salt stays well distributed. The lemons will become soft and the salt and juice mixture syrupy. Transfer the fermented jars to the refrigerator, where they will hold for up to 6 months.

To use, remove a lemon wedge and scrape off the seeds. If you see white stuff on the lemons, don't worry: it's just a precipitate of salt, oils, and whatever from the pith. I find with Meyer lemons I don't have to remove the pith before using (the flesh mostly disintegrates into syrup). Scrape the pith off regular lemons before using. For a milder taste, or if you are using quantities of preserved lemons in a dish, rinse them before cooking.

NOTE If you use regular lemons, you will need to have a few more on hand for juicing. If the lemons feel hard, soak them in room-temperature water for 15 minutes before using. To get the most juice from them, boil lemons for 2 minutes, cool, and then juice.

PRESERVED MEYER LEMON RISOTTO WITH FRIED SOFT-SHELL CRABS

For some reason risotto is one of those dishes that intimidate lots of people. They think it can be made only in a certain kind of pot, that it must be stirred constantly, with only a wooden spoon. Well, all that is nonsense. Risotto is as easy as, well, rice. And in fact, you can use regular long-grain rice for any risotto dish. It just won't be as porridgey. You can find Arborio rice, which is used in risotto, at most gourmet stores. However, if you can find riso Carnaroli, use that instead: it produces the creamiest result. (Look for brands with dates on the packages: risotto rice is best within 18 months of harvest.) Both varieties have a layer of starch that is released when the grain is heated. In combination with the broth, the starch creates a thick and creamy sauce. With the addition of a fried soft-shell crab garnish, this is one of the most sophisticated dishes I make, but it is still terrific without the crab.

3½ cups homemade or all-natural low-sodium chicken stock

2 tablespoons olive oil

1 medium onion, chopped (about 1 cup)

1½ cups riso Carnaroli or Arborio rice

½ cup dry white wine

1 Preserved Meyer Lemon, minced, plus 2 tablespoons juice from the jar

Salt and freshly ground black pepper

¼ cup grated Parmesan cheese

2 soft-shell crabs, cleaned

All-purpose flour for dredging

1 large egg, beaten

1 cup panko (Japanese bread crumbs)

Vegetable oil (not olive oil) for frying

2 tablespoons minced fresh flat-leaf parsley for garnish

SERVES 4

Pour the stock into a saucepan and heat almost to a simmer; keep warm.

Heat the olive oil in a medium heavy pot over medium heat. Add the onion, and sauté until it is wilted, about 5 minutes; do not brown. Add the rice and stir until it is well coated with oil and mixed with the onion. Cook for a minute or two. The rice will become a bit golden and want to stick to the bottom of the pan. Add the wine, loosen the rice from the bottom of the pan with a spoon, and cook until the wine is absorbed, about 5 minutes, stirring often.

Add 1 cup of the warm stock and cook until it is absorbed, about 5 minutes, stirring often. Add another cup of stock and cook until it is absorbed as well. You don't need to stir the rice forever; just keep it moving so that it doesn't stick and absorbs the stock uniformly. Continue until you have used all the stock and the rice is tender. The texture you are looking for is soft and loose, like a thick rice pudding.

Add the preserved lemon, add salt if necessary (remember, preserved lemon is salty), and add the black pepper. Stir in the cheese.

In the meantime, wash and dry the crabs. Have ready 3 shallow bowls: one with the flour, one with the beaten egg, and one with the panko. Heat the frying oil in a small skillet over medium-high heat. You will know the oil is hot enough if you flick some flour into the oil and it boils. Dredge the crabs in the flour and then dunk them in the egg and then dredge in the bread crumbs. Fry the crabs in the hot oil for a few minutes on one side, then turn and cook 1 minute or so longer until they are golden brown and crispy. Drain on paper towels. Keep warm until the risotto is ready. (I sometimes crisp the crabs up in my toaster oven before serving.)

To serve, ladle a cup of risotto into a shallow bowl. Garnish with parsley. Cut the crabs in half and stick half of a crab into each bowl of risotto, right in the middle, with the legs sticking out.

NOTE Risotto is best eaten right away. If you do make the risotto in advance, save out the last $1/2$ cup of stock and add it just before serving.

BLUEFISH WITH PRESERVED MEYER LEMON

This light, delicate dish is a great way to eat oily, or what the Italians call "green," fish. Highly nutritious, they can be a little intense. The preserved Meyer lemon, however, mediates the fish's strong taste.

2 tablespoons olive oil

1½ pounds bluefish fillet (or other oily fish like Spanish mackerel)

1 Preserved Meyer Lemon, minced, plus 2 tablespoons juice from the jar

Salt and freshly ground black pepper

SERVES 4

Preheat the broiler. Spread the olive oil in the bottom of a broiler pan. Place the fillets in the pan, skin side down. Spread the lemon and juice over the fillets and broil until the fish separates easily with a fork, about 7 minutes under an electric broiler, 5 minutes under a gas flame.

You may need a bit more preserved lemon juice if the fish looks dry. Garnish with coarsely ground black pepper. Be careful adding salt: the lemons are quite salty on their own.

CHICKEN CUTLETS WITH PRESERVED MEYER LEMON AND PARSLEY

This is a delicious dish, easy to prepare and perfect for a family dinner, but elegant enough to serve to company. I serve it with boiled potatoes rolled in parsley butter and whatever vegetable is in season.

1½ pounds chicken cutlets, about ¼ to ½ inch thick

Salt and freshly ground black pepper

All-purpose flour for dredging

2 tablespoons olive oil

2 large garlic cloves, minced

2 cups homemade or all-natural low-sodium chicken stock, warmed, or more if needed

1 Preserved Meyer Lemon, chopped, plus ¼ cup juice from the jar

3 tablespoons unsalted butter

2 tablespoons minced fresh flat-leaf parsley

SERVES 4

Season the cutlets with salt and pepper to taste (be careful with the salt—remember, preserved lemons are salty). Dredge the cutlets in flour.

Heat the oil in a large skillet over medium heat. A seasoned cast-iron or stainless-steel skillet works best, as the browned bits of chicken will help flavor the sauce. If you use a nonstick skillet, your end product will be less flavorful. Brown the cutlets in the hot oil, about 4 minutes per side. Transfer the cutlets to a plate and cover them with foil to keep them warm while you prepare the sauce.

Add the garlic to the pan you used to brown the cutlets. Sauté the garlic for a minute or two, until it becomes fragrant, but do not brown. Add the stock and the preserved lemon and juice. Loosen the brown bits with a wooden spoon and stir the ingredients together. Bring to a low boil and cook until the sauce is reduced by half, to about 1 cup, about 5 minutes. (If the sauce seems dry to you, add a little more stock.) Swirl in the butter and, when it melts, return the cutlets to the pan. Flip the cutlets in the sauce until they are warmed up and coated with sauce, just a few minutes.

Serve immediately, garnished with the parsley.

SPICED APPLES

A wide variety of apples come into the New York farmers' market in the early fall, and I am constantly experimenting with different ones. This recipe calls for Golden Delicious, but you should try it with tart apples as well. I've had great luck with Crispin, Granny Smith, and the tremendous 20 Ounce. Spiced apples are great stuffed into turnovers, piled onto potato pancakes, and folded into cake batters, among many other applications.

This recipe throws off a couple of cups of spiced apple juice. Don't throw it away! It makes a terrific granita. Just add a bit more sugar and orange juice to taste, and freeze, breaking up the ice crystals with the tines of a fork over the course of a couple of hours until you have a granulated ice.

Canned spiced apples are good for up to a year. The citric acid in them prevents the apples from browning. (They will a bit anyway—don't worry. They'll still taste great.) To figure out this recipe I used two sources, *So Easy to Preserve* and *Ball Complete Book of Home Preserving*, both of which have different, but very nice, recipes. Apples are a high-acid fruit, so they can be processed safely in a water bath. (See page 17 for information on water bath canning.)

MAKES 4 PINTS

6 pounds Golden Delicious apples
(about 24 medium)

¾ cup sugar

1 teaspoon ground cinnamon

½ teaspoon freshly grated nutmeg

¼ teaspoon ground cloves

2 teaspoons citric acid (I use Fruit Fresh)

Wash the apples. Line a colander with a thin cotton dish towel or a triple thickness of cheesecloth. Place the lined colander over a bowl. Using the large holes of a box grater, grate the apples, including the skin, into the lined colander. Grate the apples down to the core. Or peel, core, and quarter the apples and grate them in the food processor, then dump them into the cheesecloth-lined colander. Juice will start dripping through the dish towel into the bowl below. This is good. Add ¼ cup of the sugar, the cinnamon, nutmeg, and cloves on top of the grated apples and toss gently.

Gather up the dish towel and squeeze the juice out of the apples. You don't have to squeeze out every drop. This will produce about 3 cups of juice. Set aside. You will have about 8 cups of apples.

Bring 2 cups of water and the remaining ½ cup sugar to a boil in a medium pot over medium-high heat. Stir to dissolve the sugar. Add the apples and boil them in the syrup for 3 to 5 minutes.

Have ready 4 scalded pint jars and their bands. (To scald, simply dip the jars in boiling water. You don't need to sterilize the jars, as you will be pro-cessing them for over 10 minutes.) Simmer new lids in a small pan of hot water to soften the rubberized flange. Place ½ teaspoon of the citric acid in the bottom of each jar, then add the apples, leaving ½ to ¾ inch of headspace. Wipe the rims, set on the lids, and screw on the bands fingertip tight.

Place the jars on a rack in a big pot and add enough water to cover the jars by 3 inches. Cover the pot and bring to a boil over high heat, then lower the heat to medium and gently boil the jars for 25 minutes. Remove the cover and then, after about 5 minutes, remove the jars. Allow the jars to cool, untouched, for 4 to 6 hours. Check the seals and store in a cool, dark place for up to a year. Refriger-ate after opening.

In the meantime, pour the juice into a sterilized quart jar (to sterilize, boil the jar, its lid, and its band for 10 minutes) and refrigerate until you are ready to make the granita. The juice will hold in the refrigera-tor for about 3 days.

NOTE You can also substitute the water in the simple syrup with the apple juice if you don't want to bother with granita.

PORK TENDERLOIN STEAKS WITH SPICED APPLES AND THYME

Because the Spiced Apples recipe isn't super-sweet, it works well in savory recipes like this one. I love to make this dish because it is so quick and easy and everybody likes it. The dried thyme is an important flavor, so be sure what you use is less than 6 to 12 months old. Take a sniff: if the herb doesn't smell like much, it won't taste like much.

4 pork tenderloin steaks (about 1½ pounds) or pork steaks cut from the shoulder

2 scant teaspoons dried thyme

Salt and freshly ground black pepper

1 tablespoon olive oil

1 medium onion, sliced (about 1 cup)

1 pint Spiced Apples

½ cup cider vinegar

½ teaspoon dried cumin

4 sprigs fresh thyme for garnish (optional)

SERVES 4

Sprinkle the steaks with the dried thyme and salt and pepper to taste. Heat the oil in a skillet big enough to hold all 4 steaks over high heat. Add the steaks and brown them, about 3 minutes per side. Transfer the steaks to a plate and keep them warm (I prefer to cover them with foil rather than place them in a low oven).

Add the onion to the skillet you browned the steaks in and turn down the heat to medium. Cook for 5 minutes, until the onion is translucent.

Add the apples, vinegar, ½ cup of water, and the cumin. Cover and cook for about 8 minutes, until the liquid has reduced by about half. Return the steaks to the pan as well as any juices that have accumulated. Cook the steaks in the apples and onion for a few minutes, uncovered, to heat the steaks through and meld the flavors.

Serve immediately, garnished with fresh thyme if you like.

Spiced Apple Strudel

This strudel is light, fast, and delicious. I serve it for dessert with vanilla ice cream or with coffee in the morning for breakfast.

You can add raisins or dried cranberries if you like. Simply rehydrate a couple of tablespoons of the fruit in hot water, drain, and sprinkle over the bread crumb mixture. Homemade bread crumbs make the most delicate, tender strudel. The next best choice is bread crumbs produced by your local baker.

4 sheets (8 x 11 inches) phyllo pastry

5 tablespoons unsalted butter, melted

1 cup fresh bread crumbs

¼ cup sugar

1 pint Spiced Apples

1 tablespoon plus 1 teaspoon poppy seeds

Confectioners' sugar for garnish (optional)

SERVES 4

Preheat the oven to 350°F.

Lay a large piece of parchment paper on a baking sheet. Lay down the first phyllo sheet. Using a pastry brush, brush the phyllo sheet with melted butter. Lay another phyllo sheet on top and brush with butter. Continue until you have used all 4 phyllo sheets.

Combine the bread crumbs and sugar in a small bowl. Sprinkle the bread crumb mixture over the top phyllo sheet, right to the edges. Gently pat the apples over the bread crumb mixture. Sprinkle 1 tablespoon of the poppy seeds over the apples.

Carefully roll up the pastry from a long end, tucking in the sides as you near the end. (If the phyllo is a little dry, it will be difficult to tuck in the sides. Don't worry if you can't. The strudel will be fine—just not as tidy.)

Brush the top of the strudel with butter and sprinkle with the remaining teaspoon of poppy seeds.

Bake the strudel for about 40 minutes, until it is golden brown and you can smell the apples cooking. Cool the strudel to room temperature. Dust with confectioners' sugar if you like.

Wrapped in wax paper and stored in a plastic bag, the strudel will keep in the refrigerator for a couple of days. To reheat, unwrap, dot with a cut-up tablespoon of butter, and place on a tray in a 300°F oven for about 10 minutes.

SPICED APPLE PIE

If you've got a favorite piecrust recipe, by all means use it! But this one works for me.

If you want to make apple turnovers, simply buy frozen puff pastry, defrost it in the fridge, and cut it into 8-inch squares. Place a couple of tablespoons of the spiced apples in the center and then fold over the pastry to create a triangle. Press the edges to seal and bake in a 375°F oven until golden brown.

I don't have many pet peeves when it comes to cooking, but I do dislike a piece of pie that is collapsing all over the plate. I am happy to report this pie cuts perfectly.

1 cup all-purpose flour

8 tablespoons (1 stick) cold unsalted butter, chopped

2 tablespoons confectioners' sugar

Pinch of salt

2 pints Spiced Apples

2 tablespoons granulated sugar

MAKES ONE 9-INCH PIE

Preheat the oven to 350°F.

Combine the flour, butter, confectioners' sugar, and salt in a food processor and pulse to grind, until crumbly. Add 2 tablespoons cold water a tablespoon at a time until the dough comes together. As soon as it does, remove the dough, shape it into 2 patties, one large and one small, wrap in plastic wrap, and refrigerate for about 30 minutes.

Remove the large patty of dough. Roll it out on a well-floured board to a thickness of about ⅛ inch. Roll the dough up on the rolling pin and carefully lay it down over a 9-inch pie plate. Gently press the dough into place and trim the edges. Gather the trimmings into a ball and refrigerate. You'll use them for extra lattice strips if you need them.

Place the apples in the crust. You will be able to gently press them into position. Place the pie in the refrigerator.

Remove the smaller patty and roll it out on a well-floured board. Cut the dough into strips about ¾ inch wide. Remove the pie from the refrigerator and lay the strips of dough on top to create a lattice. Trim the edges and seal by pressing with the tines of a fork.

Brush about a teaspoon of water on top of the latticework and sprinkle with the granulated sugar.

Bake the pie for about 50 minutes, until the crust is golden. Allow the pie to rest for about 10 minutes before serving. This pie holds up for hours at room temperature. It refrigerates well too.

I like to serve this pie with vanilla ice cream (who the hell doesn't?).

STRAWBERRY BALSAMIC JAM

The best strawberries to use in this recipe are late June's small, sweet berries. You will have less tasty results with those large, white-hulled berries that are available throughout the year. This jam is an intense confluence of sweet and tart. Its texture is quite soft, since strawberries are low in pectin—the agent found naturally in tart fruit that makes jams and jellies stiff. Avoid overripe fruit. If the strawberries you use are very juicy, you will have extra juice left over in the pot. I either water bath can it the same way I do the jam or keep it in the refrigerator for a few days, as the juice is good for mixing into smoothies or as a fruit sauce for ice cream and rice pudding. This jam is great as a condiment for goat cheese or a topping for cheesecake.

Strawberries are high in acidity, and the balsamic vinegar is, by nature, acid, which means this product can be processed safely in a water bath. (See page 17 for information on water bath canning.)

MAKES 6 HALF-PINTS

8 cups washed and hulled strawberries (about 1½ pounds), halved if large

5 cups sugar

½ teaspoon unsalted butter

5 tablespoons balsamic vinegar

Pour the strawberries into a large, deep, heavy pot and bring to a boil over medium heat. Once the strawberries are boiling, add the sugar and stir until it is dissolved. The sugar tends to burn on the bottom, so keep it moving until it is thoroughly dissolved. Bring to a boil and then add the butter. (The addition of butter keeps the foam volume down.) Turn the heat down to medium-low and boil the jam gently for 40 minutes, until thickened to a loose, soft jam. Stir in the balsamic vinegar.

Bring 6 half-pint jars and their bands to a boil in a large pot of water fitted with a rack. Boil for 10 minutes. Remove the jars with tongs (the tongs don't need to be sterilized). Simmer new lids in a small pan of hot water, to soften the rubberized flange. When the jars are dry but still hot, use a

STRAWBERRY BALSAMIC POACHED PEARS

slotted spoon to fill the jars with the strawberries, leaving ½ to ¾ inch of headspace. Wipe the rims, set on the lids, and screw on the bands fingertip tight. You will probably have leftover juice. You can water bath can the syrup the same way you do the jam (in a sterilized jar, then a water bath process for 10 minutes), refrigerate it for around 3 days, or discard it.

Place the jars on a rack in a big pot and add enough water to cover the jars by 3 inches. Cover the pot and bring to a boil over high heat, then lower the heat to medium and gently boil the jars for 10 minutes. Remove the cover and then, after about 5 minutes, remove the jars. Allow them to rest on a dish towel for 6 hours. Check the seals and store in a cool, dark place for up to a year. Refrigerate after opening.

NOTE Sometimes I make this jam in pint jars. If you do that, process them in a water bath for 15 minutes.

STRAWBERRY BALSAMIC PANNA COTTA

Panna cotta means "cooked cream," which this isn't. But the taste is panna cotta-like—rich, smooth, and creamy—and it is excellent with balsamic strawberries.

2 teaspoons powdered gelatin

2 tablespoons boiling water

1 cup heavy cream

1 cup whole milk

¼ cup sugar

¼ teaspoon vanilla extract

¼ cup Strawberry Balsamic Jam

SERVES 4

Dissolve the gelatin in the boiling water. Be sure the gelatin is completely dissolved.

Add the cream, milk, sugar, vanilla, and dissolved gelatin to a medium saucepan and cook over medium-low heat for about 10 minutes, until the mixture is just about to boil.

Place 1 tablespoon of strawberry balsamic jam in the bottom of each of 4 ramekins. Remove the cream mixture from the heat and pour a quarter of the mixture into each ramekin. Refrigerate for 8 hours or overnight.

To serve, run a sharp knife around the perimeter of the panna cotta. Turn the ramekin over and tap abruptly onto a plate. The panna cotta should pop right out.

Rice Pudding with Strawberry Balsamic Jam

I like to serve this pudding with a dollop of jam on top and let the diner stir it in—it's nice to see the strawberries. You can substitute a teaspoon of cinnamon for the vanilla in this dish. I prefer the pudding warm, but you can chill it as well.

1 quart whole milk

½ cup sugar

1 vanilla bean, split, with seeds scraped out

1½ tablespoons unsalted butter

Pinch of salt

1 cup riso Carnaroli or Arborio rice

¼ cup Strawberry Balsamic Jam, or more if you like

SERVES 4 TO 6

Warm the milk, sugar, and vanilla bean in a medium saucepan over low heat. Do not boil.

Place 1 cup water, the butter, and salt in a medium saucepan and bring to a boil over medium heat. Add the rice. Cook until the water is absorbed, a few minutes. Add ½ cup of the warm milk. Cook the rice, stirring often, until the milk is absorbed, about 6 minutes. Add another ½ cup of milk and continue cooking until the milk is absorbed. Continue adding milk, ½ cup at a time, until all the milk is absorbed into the rice, about 30 minutes altogether, stirring frequently. The pudding is done when the rice is very tender, and you can push the rice away from the bottom of the pan. Remove the vanilla bean.

Serve the pudding with a dollop of strawberry balsamic jam on top of each serving. To chill, pour the pudding into a dish and cover with plastic wrap. The pudding stays fresh tasting for a day or so.

STRAWBERRY BALSAMIC POACHED PEARS

During the fall and winter I probably prepare poached pears more often than any other dessert. They are super-easy—foolproof, actually. The only thing you can really do wrong is overcook the pears so they become mushy and disintegrate. But beyond that, you can poach pears in anything. I always use a combination of alcohol, like wine, and a fruit juice, but the combination has varied dramatically over the years. I've poached pears in Orangina and Bordeaux, port and cider, Chardonnay and lemonade. It all works.

I prefer to serve 2 pear halves per person rather than a whole one. Serving a whole pear looks beautiful, but it is awkward to eat.

4 firm Bosc pears (Anjou are good too), peeled, halved, and seeds scooped out with a small spoon

1 cup red wine—dry, fruity, whatever

1 cup apple cider

¾ cup superfine or granulated sugar

4 sprigs fresh thyme (optional)

1 cinnamon stick, about 3 inches long

1 piece orange peel, about 2 inches long (lemon peel can be substituted)

8 whole cloves

1 half-pint jar Strawberry Balsamic Jam

SERVES 4

Place the pears, wine, cider, sugar, thyme (if using), cinnamon, orange peel, and cloves in a heavy pot with a fitted cover. Bring to a boil over medium heat, then turn the heat down to low. Simmer the pears for about 15 minutes, until they are tender when prodded with a fork. Do not overcook or they will get mushy. Allow the pears to cool in the liquid.

In the meantime, heat the strawberry balsamic jam in a small pot over low heat until it is hot, a few minutes.

Serve the pears with a couple of tablespoons of strawberry balsamic jam on top. I sometimes hit these pears with an extra dash of balsamic vinegar before serving.

THREE-CITRUS MARMALADE

This is a great marmalade to make in the winter, when the citrus comes in. It is wonderful on scones and toast or warmed up and poured over vanilla ice cream or toasted cake, but because it is not too sweet, this marmalade is terrific cooked with fish and poultry. You can use different types of oranges and lemons in this recipe (but not limes), as well as alter the lemon/orange/grapefruit ratio; the recipe will still work. You just need to follow the basic formula of 1 cup of fruit pulp to 1 cup of sugar.

Citrus fruits are, of course, high in acidity (which is why you need so much sugar), and because bacteria cannot grow in a high-acid environment, they can safely be water bath canned. Kept in a cool, dark pantry, the marmalade is good for a year. (See page 17 for more information on water bath canning.)

MAKES 4 HALF-PINTS

1 grapefruit (I prefer red)

3 oranges (blood and Honeybell are my favorites)

3 Meyer lemons

5 cups sugar

½ teaspoon unsalted butter

Peel the skin off the fruit in as big pieces as you can—I use my hands or a paring knife. Cut most of the white pith off the peels of 1 orange and 2 lemons by scraping it away with a paring knife. (Discard the remaining peels or save for other uses.) Pick off any pith remaining on the peeled fruits. It's okay if you don't get all the pith off the fruit and the rind.

Cut the reserved rinds into little matchsticks. You should have about 1 cup.

Cut the fruit in half along the equator and pop the seeds out with the tip of a paring knife. (Leaving the seeds in will give the marmalade a bitter taste—not unpleasant, but rather like Scottish-style orange marmalade.) Grind the fruit in a food processor to a chunky pulp. There should be about 5 cups. But measure the pulp you have, as there can be some variation in the amount of pulp a piece of fruit produces, and you will have to adjust the amount of sugar you add accordingly: 1 cup of sugar for every 1 cup of pulp.

In a medium pot, cover the slivered rinds with 3 cups of water. Cook over medium heat until the rinds are tender, about 25 minutes. Do not drain. Cool, then add the pulp and let it rest for 2 hours, covered, in the fridge.

Transfer the pulp, the rinds, and their cooking water to a large, wide, heavy pot. Add the sugar and the butter. (The butter helps keep the marmalade from foaming up, although it will still foam up some. The marmalade will thicken more quickly in a wide pot than a deep one. Be sure the pot is not filled more than halfway, to lessen the chances of a messy foam-up.) Cook over medium-low heat for about 30 minutes. Skim off the foam as it builds up and stir the marmalade down. The temperature must reach 220°F to jell. If you have a candy thermometer, simply stick it in the hot marmalade and rest it against the side of the pot. Place the lid on the pot to hold the thermometer in place. It will take seconds to get a reading.

If you don't have a thermometer, you can do a set test by putting a bit of the marmalade on a spoon and allowing it to cool. If the marmalade wrinkles when you push it with your finger, it is ready to can. This is a loose marmalade, but if it comes out stiff, don't worry. Just warm it up before using it in the recipes. The marmalade will darken to an amber color.

Bring 4 half-pint jars to a boil in a large pot of water fitted with a rack. Boil for 10 minutes. Remove the jars with tongs (the tongs don't need to be sterilized). Simmer new lids in a small pan of hot water to soften the rubberized flange. When the jars are dry but still hot, pour in the marmalade, leaving $\frac{1}{2}$ to $\frac{3}{4}$ inch of headspace at the top of each jar. Wipe the rims, set on the lids, and screw on the bands fingertip tight.

Place the jars in a pot fitted with a rack and add enough water to cover the jars by 3 inches. Bring the water to a boil over high heat. Process the marmalade for 10 minutes. Turn off the heat and, after about 5 minutes, remove the jars. The marmalade will seem runny at first. It's okay. It will thicken up as it cools. You will hear a popping noise as the vacuum is created in the jars. Allow the jars to sit, untouched, for 4 to 6 hours. When they are cool, test the seals. (You can test a seal by unscrewing the band and lifting the jar by the edges of the lid. If you can lift the jar, the seal is good. If the lid comes off, the seal has failed and you must reprocess the jars with new lids. Don't worry, though; the failure rate is really quite low.)

Store in a cool, dark place for up to 1 year. Refrigerate after opening.

SHRIMP WITH THREE-CITRUS MARMALADE AND LIME

In this dish shrimp are marinated for 6 hours in a sweet-and-sour marinade of marmalade and lime and lemon juice. I often set up the marinade in the morning so the shrimp are ready to go for dinner. You can also do a fast 30-minute marinade. The tart flavors won't be pronounced, but the dish will still be yummy. The shrimp are delicious served with rice but also very nice wrapped in a warm tortilla and served with an avocado salad.

3 tablespoons Three-Citrus Marmalade

2 tablespoons fresh lime juice

2 tablespoons fresh lemon juice

2 garlic cloves, minced (about 1 tablespoon)

Salt and freshly ground black pepper

1½ pounds large shrimp, peeled and deveined

1 tablespoon olive oil

3 tablespoons minced fresh cilantro

SERVES 4

Combine the marmalade, lime juice, lemon juice, garlic, and salt and pepper to taste in a large nonreactive (glass, stainless-steel, or ceramic) bowl and stir to dissolve the marmalade. Add the shrimp and toss well in the marinade. Cover with plastic wrap and refrigerate for 6 hours.

Heat the oil in a large skillet over medium heat. Using tongs, drop the shrimp into the skillet. There will be some marinade left at the bottom of the bowl—reserve it. Cook the shrimp until they turn pink, 3 to 5 minutes. Arrange the shrimp on a platter. Add the remaining marinade to the skillet and heat it until it is bubbling, about a minute. Pour the hot sauce over the shrimp and garnish with the cilantro.

CHICKEN WINGS BAKED WITH THREE-CITRUS MARMALADE

This is a variation of an Italian classic, chicken baked with honey and orange juice, which I loved as a child, and my children delight in today. Cutting a chicken into sixteenths is typical of the braised chicken dishes of Le Marche in Italy, where my father comes from. If you buy a cut-up chicken, it will probably come in eight pieces. Simply hack each thigh in half and each breast into three pieces, separate the wing and drumette, and hack off and discard the bony end of the drumsticks.

One 3½-pound chicken, cut into 16 pieces

1 half-pint jar Three-Citrus Marmalade

2 garlic cloves, minced (about 1 tablespoon)

Salt and freshly ground black pepper

SERVES 4

Preheat the oven to 400°F.

Gently combine the chicken with the marmalade, garlic, and salt and pepper to taste in a bowl. Pour into a medium baking pan and bake for 35 minutes. Turn the chicken pieces over and bake for 10 to 15 minutes longer, until the marmalade is baked on and caramelized. Serve immediately.

CRÊPES WITH THREE-CITRUS MARMALADE

This is an elegant dessert and super-easy, especially if you make the crêpes ahead of time. Just layer them between pieces of wax paper, roll them up, and set aside. You can also freeze the crêpes, packed into a freezer Baggie, for up to a month. It's quite nice to have the crêpes and marmalade on hand to dress up a supper.

¾ cup all-purpose flour

3 tablespoons sugar

1 teaspoon baking powder

Pinch of salt

2 large eggs, lightly beaten

⅔ cup whole milk

4 tablespoons (½ stick) unsalted butter

½ cup Three-Citrus Marmalade

3 tablespoons cognac

Fresh mint leaves or slivers of lemon or orange zest for garnish

SERVES 4 (ABOUT 8 CRÊPES)

In a large bowl, whisk together the flour, sugar, baking powder, and salt. In a separate bowl, whisk together the eggs, milk, and ⅓ cup of water. Add the liquid ingredients to the dry ingredients and whisk quickly, just to combine. Ignore the lumps. Refrigerate the batter for 1 hour. (More or less is okay.)

Have ready 5 sheets of wax paper about 1 foot square. Heat a crêpe pan or a small, shallow, nonstick skillet over medium-high heat. Swirl the end of a 2-tablespoon lump of cold butter around the pan, leaving a thin coating of butter. Ladle 2 tablespoons of batter into the pan and immediately tip the pan to spread the batter evenly over the bottom. Cook until air holes appear in the crêpe, about 1 minute. Flip the crêpe over and cook for 20 seconds more. Flip the crêpe onto half of a piece of wax paper. Repeat with the remaining batter and the rest of the knob of butter; place 2 crêpes on each sheet of wax paper. The first crêpe is almost always funny looking. Don't worry. There is enough batter. The pan will get progressively hotter, so moderate the temperature by either lowering the heat or taking the pan off the flame for a minute. Otherwise you will need to swirl the batter faster and faster, as it will set as soon as it hits the hot metal.

In a large, shallow saucepan, heat the marmalade over medium-low heat until it is liquid and very hot, but do not let it boil or it will begin to caramelize and burn. Fold the crêpes into quarters and add them to the marmalade. Add the cognac and the remaining 2 tablespoons butter. Shake the pan to distribute the butter. Cook until the butter is melted.

Serve immediately. This dish is very pretty garnished with mint leaves or lemon or orange zest.

TOMATILLO SAUCE

Tomatillos, which come into season in the late summer, are a tart, flavorful fruit related to the gooseberry, not the tomato. This sauce is excellent added to guacamole and salsas and as a condiment for all sorts of chile-flavored dishes. Be sure to buy tomatillos that are firm and smooth. Soft, wrinkled fruit produces a bitter sauce.

Tomatillos have a pH of less than 4.0, making them safe to water bath can. The addition of onions, chiles, and garlic, which are not acidic enough to water bath can on their own, is offset by the quantity of tomatillos and the presence of lemon juice. It is best to use bottled lemon juice, because the acidity of bottled lemon juice is more consistent than that of fresh. This is an adaptation of a recipe tested by the Michigan State University Extension. (See page 17 for information on water bath canning.)

MAKES 2 PINTS

2½ pounds tomatillos, husked and washed

2 medium mild fresh chiles (I prefer poblano and Big Jim)

1 small jalapeño chile (optional)

2 cups chopped onion

3 garlic cloves, chopped

½ cup bottled lemon juice

2 teaspoons salt

Preheat the broiler. Bring a medium pot of water to a boil.

Blanch the tomatillos in the boiling water. Do not overboil, or they will become pale and very mushy. Place them in a food processor and pulse to grind.

Place the mild and hot chiles on a baking sheet and broil for about 5 minutes, turning as they blister. Remove the chiles and, when they are cool enough to handle, remove the skins, seed pods, and veins. (Some people like to put roasted peppers in bags to loosen the skin for easy removal. I don't do it, because doing so tends to steam-cook the peppers even more.) Chop the chiles. You should have about ¾ cup.

Combine the tomatillos, chiles, onion, garlic, lemon juice, and salt in a medium pot and boil gently for 20 minutes over medium heat.

Have ready 2 scalded pint jars and their bands. (To scald, simply dip the jars in boiling water. You don't need to sterilize the jars, as you will be processing them for over 10 minutes.) Simmer new lids in a small pan of hot water to soften the rubberized flange. Ladle the sauce into the pint jars, leaving ½ to ¾ inch of headspace; wipe the rims and set on the lids. Screw on the bands fingertip tight. Place the jars in a pot fitted with a rack. Add enough water to cover the jars by 3 inches. Turn up the heat to high and bring the water to a boil. Process the jars in a boiling water bath for 15 minutes. Turn off the heat and allow the jars to rest in the water for a few minutes and then remove the jars. Allow to cool untouched for 6 to 8 hours. Check the seals and store in a cool, dark place for up to a year. Refrigerate after opening.

SCALLOP AND TOMATILLO CEVICHE

The citric acid in lime juice causes the proteins in seafood to become denatured, in effect disrupting cell activity. Ceviche is sometimes referred to as "cooked" seafood, but it only tastes that way: the fish is actually pickled.

When preparing scallops for ceviche, remove the abductor muscle. It is easy to see: a little flap on the side of the scallop that easily tears off when raw but is tough when cooked. You can substitute other fish in this recipe. Try chunks of Chilean sea bass or peeled, deveined shrimp or a combination—just be sure the pieces of fish are all about the same size so they "cook" at the same rate. You can also add ripe avocado chunks and/or thinly sliced red onion with the tomatillo.

18 sea scallops, abductor muscles removed

½ cup fresh lime juice

Salt and freshly ground black pepper

½ cup Tomatillo Sauce

¼ cup chopped fresh cilantro

2 tablespoons olive oil

Tortilla chips

SERVES 4

Combine the scallops, lime juice, and 2 teaspoons salt in a nonreactive (glass or ceramic) bowl. Cover with plastic wrap and refrigerate for 6 hours.

Drain the scallops and discard the marinade. In a serving bowl, combine the scallops, tomatillo sauce, cilantro, and olive oil. Toss. Season with salt and pepper to taste. Serve with chips.

The ceviche will hold in the refrigerator for a couple of hours.

BRIE WITH TOMATILLO SAUCE

My friend Marilee Gilman, who lives on a beautiful ranch in Hotchkiss, Colorado, is a master of the tomatillo. She cooks with it all the time. Her husband, Charlie, who is accomplished in many arts and trades including sculpture, built an adobe patio for her anchored by a tremendous—and I'm talking 12-foot-high—seated naked lady with a fireplace between her legs. This is where they like to serve cocktails, and it's where I first tasted this really delicious concoction.

½ pound Brie, a small round or a big wedge (I like d'Affinois)

½ cup Tomatillo Sauce

Tortilla chips

SERVES 4

Place the Brie on a serving platter. Allow it to come to room temperature. If it starts to melt and run, that's good. Dump the tomatillo sauce over it. Serve with chips.

CORN AND TOMATILLO SOUP

This is an adaptation of a corn soup prepared by Bob Isaacson, the former chef at the Smith Fork Ranch in Crawford, Colorado. This soup is good served hot or at room temperature.

3 tablespoons olive oil

1 large onion, finely chopped (about 1½ cups)

4 garlic cloves, finely chopped (about 2 tablespoons)

6 ears fresh corn, kernels cut off (about 4 cups), plus the cobs

2 cups homemade or all-natural low-sodium chicken stock

1 bay leaf

Salt and freshly ground black pepper

½ cup heavy cream or half-and-half

4 heaping tablespoons Tomatillo Sauce

4 teaspoons chopped fresh flat-leaf parsley

SERVES 4

Heat the oil in a soup pot over medium heat. Add the onion and garlic and sauté until the onion is translucent, about 5 minutes. Snap the corn cobs in half and put them in the pot. Add enough water just to cover—as soon as the cobs float, you've got enough. Boil the cobs, covered, for 30 minutes. Remove the cobs with tongs and discard. Add the chicken stock and bay leaf to the soup pot. Bring to a gentle boil and cook, uncovered, for about 15 minutes, until the stock is reduced by about a third. You can store the stock in the fridge at this point, refrigerate the kernels, and finish the soup later.

Add the corn kernels and boil gently over medium-low heat until they are tender, about 5 minutes. Add salt to taste. Remove the bay leaf. Stir in the cream, but do not cook the soup any longer. (Simmering is okay if you want to serve it very hot.) Swirl in the tomatillo sauce, either into the soup pot or into each individual serving bowl. Garnish with chopped parsley and black pepper.

NOTE You can puree this soup if you like. Before adding the cream, puree 2 cups of the soup at a time in your food processor or blender. You can also push the soup through a food mill or China cap, for a very smooth result.

CHICKEN AND TOMATILLO STEW

This is a highly flavored dish that balances tart and warm flavors very nicely. It is wonderful with a bowl of basmati or saffron rice and a spicy white wine like Gewürztraminer. The stew holds well in the refrigerator, but the sauce thickens up, so add a little warm chicken stock when you reheat it.

1 tablespoon olive oil

1 whole chicken breast, cut into 4 pieces, and 4 small thighs (about 2 pounds total)

Salt and freshly ground black pepper

½ teaspoon ground cumin

½ teaspoon sweet paprika

½ teaspoon grated lemon zest

¼ teaspoon ground cinnamon

1 pint Tomatillo Sauce

1¼ cups homemade or all-natural low-sodium chicken stock

3 tablespoons minced fresh cilantro for garnish

SERVES 4

Heat the oil in a 3- to 4-quart Dutch oven or heavy pan with a fitted lid over medium-high heat. Season the chicken with salt and pepper to taste and brown it in the oil for about 10 minutes, until it is browned all over (depending on the size of the pot, you may have to brown the chicken in batches). If the chicken throws off a lot of fat, spoon some out, leaving just a few tablespoons in the bottom of the pan.

Add the cumin, paprika, lemon zest, and cinnamon and stir to coat the chicken well. Add the tomatillo sauce and the chicken stock. Bring to a boil over medium heat, lower the heat to medium-low, cover, and cook the stew at a low boil for 45 to 60 minutes, until the chicken is very tender and the sauce fragrant. Uncover the pot and continue cooking for about 15 minutes to reduce the sauce by about a third. Check the seasoning.

Serve the chicken with rice, if you like, and garnish with the cilantro.

VEGETABLES

PICKLED ASPARAGUS

These asparagus are tangy and tender, and their addition to a dish really pumps up the intensity. They are also quite pretty and make a lovely first course, served whole with a dollop of homemade mayonnaise. Beyond that, they are a wonderful substitute for capers and great in composed salads. You can find asparagus year-round, but they really are best in their season, spring. Asparagus are low in acidity, but since these asparagus are pickled (preserved in a high-acid solution), they are safe to water bath process. After a four-week seasoning period, these will be good for a year. (See pages 17 and 24 for information on water bath processing and pickling.)

MAKES 3 PINTS

5 pounds asparagus

2¼ cups distilled white or white wine vinegar with 5 percent acidity

¼ cup pickling salt

2 garlic cloves, slivered (about 1 tablespoon)

1 teaspoon dill seed

½ teaspoon hot red pepper flakes

¼ teaspoon whole allspice berries (optional)

¼ teaspoon cumin seeds (optional)

¼ teaspoon coriander seeds (optional)

Trim the asparagus to fit very snugly standing upright in a pint jar. The tips must not penetrate into the rim area of the jar, so you will have to cut them quite short. I end up cutting at least 3 inches off the bottoms, which I save for another use—to make cream of asparagus soup, for example. Jersey Giants, the purple-topped asparagus, by the way, are delicious and meaty, but they will stain the vinegar solution. It's okay.

Place about 2 inches of water in a shallow pan large enough to hold the asparagus. Bring to a boil over medium-high heat. Lay enough asparagus to fit into the pint jars in the pan, plus a few extra, and bring the water back to a boil. Remove the asparagus and run them under very cold water or dunk them in ice water. This sets the green color. Set aside.

Combine the vinegar, salt, garlic, dill seed, and hot red pepper flakes, and, if you like, the allspice, cumin, and/or coriander in a saucepan with 2¼ cups water and bring to a boil over medium heat. Stir to dissolve the salt. Do not boil past the point where the salt has dissolved. Acetic acid evaporates faster than water, and overboiling can upset the water-to-vinegar ratio.

Boil 3 pint jars in a large pot of water fitted with a rack for 10 minutes. Simmer new lids in a small pan of hot water to soften the rubberized flange. When the jars are dry but still hot, pack the asparagus into them upright. You really have to wedge the asparagus in, or they will bob above the rim once you add the vinegar solution.

Fill the jars with the vinegar solution, enough to cover the tops of the asparagus. Allow another ½ to ¾ inch of headspace above the vinegar solution. Distribute the spices among the jars. Wipe the rims, set on the lids, and screw on the bands fingertip tight.

Place the jars in a pot fitted with a rack and cover the jars with 2 to 3 inches of water. Bring the water to a boil over high heat, then lower the heat to medium and gently boil the jars for 10 minutes. Turn off the heat, allow the jars to rest in the water for 5 minutes or so, and then remove. Allow the jars to cool, untouched, for 4 to 6 hours. Don't leave the jars in the water to cool, or the asparagus will overcook and become pale and withered. As is, they will yellow a bit and will float in the vinegar, as they shrink some during processing. Both of these occurrences are okay.

Allow the asparagus to season in a cool, dark place for 4 weeks, after which they will be good for a year. Refrigerate after opening.

PICKLED ASPARAGUS WITH EGGS

When someone drops by unexpectedly and I have to stretch a dinner, I will usually prepare an additional course. This classic is an excellent and fast first course and is suitable before every entrée I can think of. You can add a further garnish of minced fresh herbs, like parsley, cilantro, or chives.

6 hard-cooked eggs

12 Pickled Asparagus spears

Extra virgin olive oil

Salt and freshly ground black pepper

SERVES 4 AS AN APPETIZER

Peel the eggs and slice or chop. Arrange the asparagus on serving plates and sprinkle the egg on top. Dribble with extra virgin olive oil, enough to make the dish glisten, and season to taste.

SKATE WING WITH PICKLED ASPARAGUS

Skate is a delicious, inexpensive fish in the ray family. The bones in the skate wing are cartilaginous: soft and large. They do not have to be removed. Each diner gently scrapes the meat off the bone with the tines of his fork. This cut of fish is gelatinous—and that means it's sweet! Serving skate wing with browned butter and pickled asparagus is not only delicious but adds a bit of surprise to the bistro standby, skate wing with capers. If the wings are small, leave them be, but if your fishmonger is selling very large wings, cut them into 4 equal serving pieces.

2 cups fish stock or water

2 tablespoons white wine vinegar, champagne vinegar, or white sherry vinegar

12 peppercorns

2 sprigs each fresh flat-leaf parsley and fresh thyme or 4 of either one

1 bay leaf

Salt and freshly ground black pepper

1½ pounds skate wing

8 tablespoons (1 stick) unsalted butter

12 Pickled Asparagus spears, cut into 1-inch pieces, plus about 1 tablespoon liquid from the jar

SERVES 4

Place the fish stock, vinegar, peppercorns, fresh herbs, bay leaf, and salt to taste in a wide, shallow sauté pan with a tight-fitting lid. This mixture is called a *court bouillon*. Bring the court bouillon to a gentle boil over medium heat. Add the skate wing and poach until the flesh pulls easily away from the bone, 5 minutes for every ½ inch thickness of fish. Drain the cooked wings, sprinkle with salt, and place them on a serving platter.

In a small skillet, melt the butter over medium-low heat. Cook until the butter browns, a few minutes. Add the asparagus and the pickling juices. Heat the asparagus through, about 2 minutes, then pour the browned butter and asparagus mixture over the skate wing. Garnish with freshly ground black pepper. Serve immediately.

CHICKEN PICCATA WITH PICKLED ASPARAGUS

This ubiquitous trattoria dish is very easy to make. The addition of asparagus makes it unique. In the winter, when the Meyer lemons are in, try them in this dish. They add a sweeter citrus flavor than standard lemons. Do not substitute limes—they aren't as tasty here. You can prepare this dish in a nonstick skillet, but you won't get those delicious browned bits. Better to use stainless steel or cast iron.

2 large lemons

1½ pounds chicken scaloppine

Salt and freshly ground black pepper

¼ cup all-purpose flour

¼ cup olive oil

2 garlic cloves, minced (about 1 tablespoon)

1½ cups warm homemade or all-natural low-sodium chicken stock

3 tablespoons unsalted butter

8 Pickled Asparagus spears, cut into pieces about 1 inch long

2 tablespoons minced fresh flat-leaf parsley for garnish

SERVES 4

Cut half of one lemon into thin slices, pole to pole. Juice the remaining half and the other lemon. You should have about 5 tablespoons of juice.

Season the cutlets with salt and pepper to taste. Place the flour in a shallow bowl and dredge the cutlets in the flour. Heat 2 tablespoons of the oil in a medium-large skillet over medium heat. Add half the cutlets and sauté until lightly browned, about 4 minutes on each side. Transfer the browned cutlets to a platter and cover with foil. Add the remaining oil to the skillet and cook the remaining cutlets. The cutlets should be just cooked through.

Add the garlic to the empty skillet and cook until soft, about 1 minute. Add the stock and lemon slices and bring to a light boil, scraping the bottom of the pan with a wooden spoon to loosen the browned bits. Reduce the sauce by about half, 5 minutes or so, and then turn off the heat. Add the butter and stir to melt, and then add the asparagus. Add the cutlets to the skillet, turning them over in the sauce until they are well covered and warm. Serve immediately, garnished with the parsley.

MARINATED BABY ARTICHOKES

These are so convenient to have on hand. Less greasy than commercial products, they are superb tossed with chopped boiled shrimp or on a pizza with fontina cheese. Lots of home cooks in France and Italy prepare marinated artichokes, including my Zia Ada in Le Marche, but there are no laboratory-tested recipes that I could base mine on. I tormented one poor food scientist for a week about how to make this recipe safe, until, exasperated, she explained how she tested recipes—make a slurry of the product and use a digital pH meter to test the pH. I then went on to torment the poor folks at Cole-Parmer Instrument Company with questions about my meter's accuracy. In the end, the final acidity of these artichokes is pH 3.5, well within the safety limits for water bath canning. (You have to use bottled lemon juice, because the acidity is more consistent than that of fresh. It's a bummer, but true.) The processing time is based on the recommended time for marinated peppers, which also contain more than 2 tablespoons of olive oil per pint (the maximum amount that can be added to a product without affecting processing times).

Baby artichokes are traditionally a spring vegetable, although I have found them at my local farmers' market in New York through August. The artichokes need to season for about two weeks, and will keep for up to a year. (See page 17 for more information about water bath canning.)

MAKES 4 PINTS

48 baby artichokes the size of a child's fist
(about 6 pounds)

1 cup bottled lemon juice

2 cups white wine vinegar with
5 percent acidity

1 cup olive oil

2 garlic cloves, sliced (about 1 tablespoon)

2 teaspoons salt

2 bay leaves

Remove the tough outer leaves of the artichokes, reducing the volume of the vegetable by half, until each artichoke has the shape of a teardrop or candle flame, is pale green to yellow, and is soft to the touch. With a paring knife, trim the base, removing all the rough surfaces. Cut the artichokes in half and pluck out any thistly interior leaves.

In a large nonreactive pot, combine the lemon juice, vinegar, oil, garlic, salt, and bay leaves and bring to a boil. Add the artichokes and boil for 10 minutes. Remove the bay leaves.

Have ready 4 scalded pint jars and their bands. (To scald, simply dip the jars in boiling water. You don't need to sterilize the jars, as you will be processing them for over 10 minutes.) Simmer new lids in a small pan of hot water, to soften the rubberized flange. When the jars are dry but still hot, remove the artichokes from the marinade with a slotted spoon and pack them into the jars, filling the jars about three-quarters full. Resist the temptation to overpack or you will compromise your seal. Cover the artichokes with the marinade, distributing the garlic evenly and leaving ½ to ¾ inch of headspace. Wipe the rims, set on the lids, and screw on the bands fingertip tight.

Place the jars in a pot fitted with a rack and add enough water to cover the jars by 3 inches. Cover the pot and bring the water to a boil over high heat. Process the artichokes for 25 minutes. Turn off the heat and remove the lid. After a few minutes, remove the artichokes.

Allow the jars to cool completely before checking the seals. Allow the artichokes to season for 2 weeks before using, after which they'll keep in a cool, dark place for about a year. Once opened, keep in the refrigerator.

ARTICHOKE GRATIN

I tasted this dish at a wonderful restaurant called Epicurean in Steamboat Springs, Colorado. The recipe was created by Epicurean's owner and chef, Rebecca Pauvert (her husband, Marcel, prepares the charcuterie: it's top-notch). This is very rich and tasty—delectable, actually. I almost always make my own mayonnaise, but as this recipe calls for 3 cups, I spare my biceps and buy an all-natural canola oil mayo at the health food store. It works perfectly.

6 garlic cloves, minced (about 3 tablespoons)

6 tablespoons olive oil

1 pint Marinated Baby Artichokes, drained

3 cups mayonnaise

1 cup sour cream

2 cups Gruyère cheese grated on the large holes of a box grater (about ½ pound)

SERVES 6 AS AN APPETIZER

Preheat the oven to 250°F.

In a small pot, simmer the garlic and olive oil together over low heat for 15 to 20 minutes, until the garlic is golden. Drain the garlic and set aside. (You can use the olive oil again, but it must be refrigerated.)

Dump the artichokes onto a baking sheet and bake for about 20 minutes to dry them out. With scissors, snip the artichokes in half. Combine the artichokes and garlic in a small bowl and let them marinate for about 20 minutes.

Turn the oven up to 350°F.

In a large bowl, whisk together the mayonnaise and sour cream. Fold in the cheese. Add the artichoke and garlic mixture and combine well.

Pour the gratin mixture into 6 individual ramekins. Place the ramekins on a baking sheet and bake for about 20 minutes, until the gratins are golden brown and bubbling. Serve hot with crusty French bread.

RICOTTA PIE WITH MARINATED BABY ARTICHOKES

This is a typical country Italian dish in that it is very elegant yet rustic and unpretentious. I make it when I know people are coming by, but don't know exactly when, as it sits around very happily for quite a few hours. It's also a favorite dish of our plumber, George.

FOR THE PASTRY

2 cups all-purpose flour

2 large eggs

8 tablespoons (1 stick) cold unsalted butter

1 teaspoon warm water

½ teaspoon active dry yeast

½ teaspoon salt

FOR THE FILLING

2 pounds fresh ricotta cheese (two 15-ounce containers)

¼ pound boiled ham, cubed (about 1 cup)

½ pint Marinated Baby Artichokes, drained and chopped

2 large egg whites

3 tablespoons chopped fresh flat-leaf parsley

½ teaspoon freshly grated nutmeg

Salt and freshly ground black pepper

ONE 9-INCH PIE

Preheat the oven to 350°F. Butter a deep 9-inch pie plate.

Make the crust. Place the flour and eggs in a food processor. Cut the butter into little pieces, add, and pulse to combine. Combine the water and yeast in a small cup and add it to the flour mixture. Add the salt. Process the dough for about 45 seconds, until it forms a ball or many small balls.

Dump the dough out onto your work surface and form it into 2 separate patties, one a little larger than the other. Wrap the dough patties in wax paper and let them rest in the refrigerator for 30 minutes.

In a large bowl, stir together the ricotta, ham, artichokes, egg whites, parsley, nutmeg, and salt and pepper to taste.

On a lightly floured work surface, roll out the larger dough patty by pressing in the center with your rolling pin and slowly rolling outward in all directions. Place the dough in the pie plate. Pour the ricotta and artichoke mixture into the crust.

Roll out the remaining dough patty and place the crust over the filling. Crimp the edges to seal and cut a few slashes in the top crust. Brush the top of the crust with a little water or beaten egg and bake for 1 hour, until the crust is golden brown.

Serve immediately or in a few hours. Wrapped carefully, it holds up well in the fridge overnight.

SAUSAGES WITH MARINATED BABY ARTICHOKES

My dad developed this recipe. He loves marinated artichokes, which his mother and his aunt made every year. He cooks these sausages in parchment paper, which is available at most grocery stores, but the dish works equally well if you simply sauté the sausages until they are brown and cooked through, then discard any residual fat. I serve this dish with big hunks of Italian bread. Indeed, the sausage and artichokes make a terrific sandwich.

4 medium-size sweet Italian sausages

Hot red pepper flakes (optional)

1 pint Marinated Baby Artichokes, drained

Salt and freshly ground black pepper

2 tablespoons minced fresh flat-leaf parsley

SERVES 2

Preheat the oven to 450°F.

Puncture the sausages with a fork. Sprinkle the sausages with hot red pepper flakes to taste and roll them up in parchment paper. Place the sausages in a baking dish and bake for about 20 minutes, until the sausages are cooked through.

Remove the sausages from the parchment and cut them on the bias into 1-inch sections.

Dump the artichokes into a saucepan and heat them over medium heat until they are hot and any liquid is bubbling. Add the sausages and combine. Serve hot or at room temperature, garnished with parsley.

PICKLED CAULIFLOWER

I love these pickles. They are a beautiful element in a composed salad, delicious next to a plate of broiled squid, excellent cooked with tomatoes and olives as a side dish, wonderful served with bread and butter and a dozen raw oysters. Cauliflower is a low-acid vegetable, and so to water bath can it safely, the acidity must be increased through pickling. In choosing cauliflower, which is a fall vegetable, select very fresh, tight white florets without brown spots. If the finished pickled cauliflower takes on a pinkish color, it may be because the vegetable was overmature when it was pickled. Sometimes the cauliflower will discolor even if it is very fresh, a reaction to the vinegar solution. Either way, it is totally safe to eat. This recipe is adapted from the Michigan State University Extension's database "Preserving Food Safely." (See pages 24 and 17 for information on pickling and water bath canning.) These pickles are good for up to a year.

MAKES 6 PINTS

Pickling salt

2½ pounds cauliflower, broken into florets (about 12 cups)

1 quart white wine vinegar, distilled white vinegar, or a combination (with 5 percent acidity)

2 cups sugar

2 medium onions, thinly sliced (about 2 cups)

½ teaspoon hot red pepper flakes, or more to taste

Bring a large pot of water to a boil over high heat. Add ¼ cup of pickling salt to every gallon of water in the pot. Drop in the cauliflower florets and boil them for about 3 minutes. Drain.

In a medium nonreactive pot, combine the vinegar, sugar, onions, and hot red pepper flakes. Swirl until the sugar dissolves. Bring to a boil over medium heat and boil gently for 5 minutes. Remove from the heat.

Bring 6 pint jars and their bands to a boil in a large pot of water fitted with a rack. Boil for 10 minutes. Remove the jars with tongs (the tongs don't need to be sterilized). Simmer new lids in a small pan of hot water to soften the rubberized flange. When the jars are dry but still hot, gently pack the cauliflower and the onions into the jars. Don't shove, as you want the florets to retain their shape.

Cover the vegetables with the vinegar solution, making sure the hot red pepper flakes are distributed well throughout. Allow ½ to ¾ inch of headspace above the vinegar solution. Wipe the rims, set on the lids, and screw on the bands fingertip tight.

Place the jars in a pot fitted with a rack and add enough water to cover the jars by 3 inches. Bring the water to a boil over high heat. Process the cauliflower for 10 minutes. Turn off the heat and let the jars sit for a few minutes and then remove them from the water. (They'll be hot, so if you don't have a jar lifter, pour out some of the boiling water and grab the jars using an oven mitt.) Don't leave the jars in the water to cool, or the cauliflower will overcook.

Allow the cauliflower to season in a cool, dark place for 4 weeks before using it, after which it will keep for up to a year. Refrigerate after opening.

PENNE WITH GROUND PORK AND CAULIFLOWER

This is not particularly saucy. Should you find you miss that terribly, you can add an extra cup of warm stock to the ground pork to produce a sort of gravy.

1 tablespoon olive oil

1 tablespoon minced garlic

1 pound ground pork (see Note)

½ cup dry white wine

2 teaspoons fresh thyme leaves or 1 teaspoon dried

Salt and freshly ground black pepper

½ cup homemade or all-natural low-sodium beef or chicken stock, plus more as needed

¾ pound cut pasta, like penne or rigatoni

1 pint Pickled Cauliflower, drained

½ cup grated Parmesan cheese

2 tablespoons minced fresh flat-leaf parsley

Extra virgin olive oil for garnish

SERVES 4

Heat 1 tablespoon olive oil in a large saucepan over medium heat. Turn the heat down to medium-low and add the garlic. Cook for about 2 minutes, until the garlic becomes fragrant. Add the pork and brown, stirring frequently to break up the clumps, for 5 to 7 minutes. Add the wine, thyme, and salt and pepper to taste. Cook until the wine evaporates, 3 to 4 minutes. Add the stock, cover, and cook for about 6 minutes, until the pork is moist, crumbly, and thoroughly cooked.

In the meantime, bring a large pot of salted water to a boil over high heat. Add the pasta and cook until it is al dente. Drain.

Add the penne to the pork and combine well. Stir in the pickled cauliflower and combine. If the pasta seems very dry, add a bit more warm stock to loosen it up. Check the seasoning.

Pour the pasta onto a serving platter and garnish with cheese, parsley, a dribble of extra virgin olive oil, and a few more grinds of black pepper.

NOTE I buy pork loin with a nice strip of fat on it and ask the butcher to grind it up. The result is fluffier and fresher tasting than preground pork.

POACHED FISH SALAD WITH PICKLED CAULIFLOWER

I was so excited when I first stumbled on this dish—I think it is very elegant. You can replace or augment the halibut with large shrimp, Chilean sea bass, or big sea scallops. All work well. You can also dress it in different ways, playing around with fresh herbs, minced red onions, red peppercorns, chopped avocado, thin strips of red and green bell peppers, cold leftover boiled corn kernels. . . .

3 sprigs fresh thyme

3 sprigs fresh flat-leaf parsley

1 bay leaf

10 peppercorns

1½ pounds halibut fillet (about 2 inches thick), cut into large pieces

2 pints Pickled Cauliflower

4 hard-cooked eggs, peeled and cut into wedges

1 to 2 tablespoons extra virgin olive oil

Salt and freshly ground black pepper

2 tablespoons minced fresh flat-leaf parsley

SERVES 4

Place the thyme, parsley, bay leaf, and peppercorns in a saucepan with 3 cups of water. Bring to a gentle boil over medium-high heat. Add the halibut. The water should come about halfway up the sides of the fish. Cover the pan and poach the fish for about 7 minutes, then gently turn it over and cook for 6 minutes more, until the flesh is opaque throughout and separates easily when prodded with the tines of a fork. Transfer the fish to a plate and cool to room temperature.

Drain the pickled cauliflower. Cut the halibut into bite-sized pieces that are on the large side.

On a deep serving platter, gently toss the halibut and cauliflower together. Add the eggs. Dress with a dribble of extra virgin olive oil, season with salt and pepper to taste, and garnish with the parsley.

CHICKEN WITH PICKLED CAULIFLOWER

This is an adaptation of a dish I ate often as a child, chicken with cauliflower and vinegar. It was tart and tasty. Still is.

4 chicken thighs

1 whole chicken breast, cut into 4 pieces

Salt and freshly ground black pepper

2 tablespoons olive oil

2 large fresh tomatoes, chopped, or 2½ cups canned whole tomatoes, drained and chopped

2 pints Pickled Cauliflower

1 cup homemade or all-natural low-sodium chicken stock, warmed, if needed

2 tablespoons minced fresh flat-leaf parsley

SERVES 4

Season the chicken pieces with salt and pepper to taste. Heat the oil in a medium skillet over medium heat. Add the chicken pieces and cook until browned all over, about 30 minutes. Remove the chicken pieces; place them on a platter and cover with foil to keep them warm. Pour off the excess oil and fat, leaving about 1 tablespoon in the bottom of the pan. Add the tomatoes to the pan and cook for about 5 minutes, until they soften.

Drain the pickled cauliflower and dump it into the skillet with the tomatoes. If the tomatoes are not giving off enough juice to make a light sauce, add the warm chicken stock. Cook the tomatoes and cauliflower together for about 5 minutes. The vinegar smell will be strong at first, then less so. Add the chicken pieces and whatever juices may have accumulated in the bottom of the platter. Cook, covered, for 5 minutes over medium-low heat, until the chicken is hot and the sauce bubbling.

Serve immediately, garnished with parsley.

PRESERVED ZUCCHINI

It is an absolute delight to have these preserved zucchini in the fridge, and I do all summer, when the zucchini are best. They are very delicious and versatile: you can throw them into a cold, creamy soup or blanket a piece of fish with chopped preserved zucchini and bake or even make quick, tasty bruschetta. Choose the zucchini carefully: you want them fresh, firm, and market size (about 8 inches long). Avoid those baseball bat–sized zucchini, which are seedy and get mushy when you cook them.

Here the zucchini are broiled, which kills most spoilers, and then covered in oil, which shields the zucchini from additional spoilers that may be in your fridge as well as inhibiting the growth of most spoilers that may have survived the cooking process. The zucchini is then refrigerated, which retards the growth of spoilers. It is good for 10 days. (See page 37 for information on preserving in oil.)

MAKES 1½ POUNDS

3 pounds market-size zucchini (about 8), cut into planks (not rounds, which seem to cook up wetter) about ¼ inch thick

3 tablespoons minced fresh flat-leaf parsley (optional)

4 garlic cloves, minced (about 2 tablespoons)

Salt and freshly ground black pepper

Olive oil to cover

Place the oven rack about 6 inches below the heating element. (If the zucchini is broiled too close to the flame, it will burn. As it is, it will blister.) Preheat the broiler.

Lightly oil a baking sheet. Arrange the zucchini planks on the baking sheet and broil for 5 to 7 minutes, until browned on top. Then turn the zucchini over and broil the second side for 2 to 3 minutes more, until browned. (You can also grill the zucchini.)

Remove the zucchini as it is done and let it rest on paper towels while you finish broiling. (Some pieces will take longer than others, due to your stove or the thickness of the planks.) The zucchini will release some juice. This is good—you want them to dry out a little.

When all the zucchini are done, lay one layer down in a small square storage container or glass pan. Sprinkle with parsley, garlic, and salt and black pepper to taste. Make several more layers, seasoning each. Once all the zucchini are in, cover them with oil, put on the top or cover with plastic wrap, and refrigerate right away. Avoid letting the zucchini sit at room temperature covered in oil, as spoilers may bloom, and the zucchini will absorb too much oil. The oil should harden quickly in the fridge.

To use, just peel off the strips of zucchini from the cold oil as you need them and re-cover the remaining zucchini with oil. I chop the zucchini with the cold oil clinging to it. Re-cover the remaining zucchini with oil and refrigerate immediately. If you find the zucchini are very oily, dab them with paper towels before using.

Preserved Zucchini and Mozzarella Hors d'Oeuvres

I make these quick hors d'oeuvres all summer long, and my company loves them. Be careful about using very soft buffalo mozzarella in this recipe. As it warms up, it releases some of its milk, making for messy finger food. If you can get them, mozzarella balls the size of marbles are ideal. Tiny marinated mozzarella balls are good too, but you should roll them around on a paper towel first to remove some of the oil. Usually the mozzarella is about the size of Ping-Pong balls, so cut them in half. Mozzarella balls are sold in water.

12 slices Preserved Zucchini

6 mozzarella balls about the size of Ping Pong balls, drained and cut in half

12 small fresh basil leaves (optional)

Salt and freshly ground black pepper

SERVES 4

Peel the zucchini planks out of their container and bring them to room temperature. If they seem very oily, dab with a paper towel.

Roll a piece of mozzarella and a basil leaf in a zucchini plank. Fasten with a toothpick. Garnish with a light sprinkle of salt and a few grinds of black pepper (but taste one first: the preserved zucchini already have salt in them).

NOTE For another simple hors d'oeuvre, chop the preserved zucchini and spoon onto little rounds of toasted baguette for preserved zucchini bruschetta.

Pasta with Preserved Zucchini and Tomatoes

I serve this very quick and tasty dish for a light dinner during the summer when the tomatoes are in.

6 cups homemade or all-natural low-sodium chicken stock

¾ pound spaghettini or linguine fini

½ pound Preserved Zucchini (about 4 cups chopped)

Salt and freshly ground black pepper

2 large fresh tomatoes at room temperature, chopped (about 2 cups)

½ cup grated Parmesan cheese

SERVES 4

Bring the stock to a low boil over medium heat. Add the pasta, stirring frequently to make sure it doesn't stick. The pasta will absorb the stock, and the starch in the pasta will thicken it. Cook until al dente.

In the meantime, remove the zucchini from the oil and chop coarsely. Don't worry about the oil on it—you'll use that rather than adding oil to the dish. Toss the zucchini in a medium skillet over medium heat. When the oil is melted and the zucchini are hot, after about 5 minutes, remove from the heat.

Throw the zucchini into the pot with the cooked pasta. The sauce (the thickened chicken stock) should be loose and creamy. Toss the zucchini and pasta together to combine well. Check the seasoning. It may not need salt, but a few grinds of black pepper will be delicious.

Pour the spaghetti onto a platter and garnish with the fresh tomatoes and grated cheese. Serve immediately. (Pasta cooked in stock does not like to sit around—it can get a bit gummy when cool.)

SHRIMP AND PRESERVED ZUCCHINI SALAD

This salad is terrific, and to boot, it spins off two other tasty recipes, so I make a point of preparing more than I need. With the leftovers, I snip each shrimp into three pieces with kitchen scissors and toss them and the zucchini mixture into soft scrambled eggs. You can also warm the snipped shrimp and zucchini mixture in a skillet over low heat with a tablespoon of gently sautéed minced garlic. Add a tablespoon of minced flat-leaf parsley and another of minced basil, plus a cup of white wine, and cook until they are all heated through. Then add 3/4 pound of cooked spaghettini, and garnish with grated Parmesan. When I have it on hand, I garnish the pasta with a couple tablespoons of grated bottarga (smoked red mullet roe). Both are very sexy dishes.

You can substitute or add grilled scallops. Chunks of grilled fresh tuna or swordfish are good too.

24 jumbo shrimp

1/2 pound Preserved Zucchini (about 4 cups chopped)

2 garlic cloves, minced (about 1 tablespoon)

1 teaspoon fresh lemon juice

Salt and freshly ground black pepper

SERVES 4

Peel and devein the shrimp and boil them in water for a few minutes, until pink. Drain and chill in the refrigerator (see Note).

Remove the zucchini planks and chop. Do not worry about the hardened oil on them. Place in a serving bowl and allow to rest at room temperature until the oil melts.

Toss the lightly chilled shrimp, garlic, lemon juice, and chopped zucchini together until the flavors are melded. Add salt and pepper to taste. Serve right away or refrigerate: the salad is excellent the next day.

NOTE Avoid serving the shrimp ice-cold. It undermines the flavor.

MARINATED RED BELL PEPPERS

I always make this recipe in the fall, when peppers are in season and inexpensive. Heavily refrigerated peppers may look smooth and hard on the outside, but their inferiority is evident when you broil them and the flesh cooks up slippery and soft. The taste is affected too: it's not as sweet. Marinated peppers are an antipasto mainstay. I like to toss the peppers with tuna, boiled shrimp, or grilled scallops and garnish with parsley.

This makes a brothy marinade with a 3.5 to 4.0 pH, well within the range where spoilers can't grow. It is adapted from a recipe circulated by the Michigan State University Extension. You may find that after a month or two of shelf time, when you open the can the top pepper may be a little softer than the others. You can use it or chuck it, at your discretion. The remainder of the peppers will be great. The peppers are good for up to a year. (See page 17 for more information about water bath canning.)

MAKES 3 PINTS

4 pounds red bell peppers (8 to 10 medium), stems snipped off

1 cup bottled lemon juice

2 cups white wine vinegar with 5 percent acidity

1 cup olive oil

2 medium garlic cloves, sliced (about 1 tablespoon)

1½ teaspoons salt

Place the oven rack about 7 inches from the broiler and preheat the broiler. Place the peppers on a baking sheet and char them under the broiler, turning them often with tongs so that they blister all over, about 20 minutes. Let the peppers stand until cool enough to handle. Remove the charred skin, cut the peppers in half, and remove the seed pods.

Combine the lemon juice, vinegar, olive oil, garlic, and salt in a saucepan and heat just to boiling over medium heat.

Have ready 3 scalded pint jars and their bands. (To scald, simply dip the jars in boiling water. You don't need to sterilize the jars, as you will be processing them for over 10 minutes.) Simmer new lids in a small pan of hot water to soften the rubberized flange.

Pack the peppers into the jars and pour the marinade over them. Using a butter knife, pop any air bubbles in the jars. See that the garlic slices are distributed evenly. Be sure to leave ½ to ¾ inch of headspace in the jars, or your seal might fail. (Why? Because the peppers puff up some during the water bath process, and if there is not enough space for the air to be pushed out of the jar by the heat, the pressure will push out oil as well and the seals won't stick.) Wipe the rims, place on the lids, and screw on the bands fingertip tight.

Process the peppers in a boiling water bath for 15 minutes. Turn off the heat and allow the jars to sit in the water for 5 minutes, then remove the jars and let them rest for 4 to 6 hours. Check the seals and store in a cool, dry place for up to a year.

Baccalà and Marinated Red Bell Pepper Salad

Baccalà—salted codfish—and stockfish must be soaked in fresh water for 2 to 4 days before cooking, at which point the fish loses its strong salty taste and becomes mild and flavorful.

1 pound salt cod or stockfish

2 large garlic cloves, peeled and smashed with the flat side of a cook's knife

5 small potatoes (I like baby Yukon Gold), peeled

½ pint Marinated Red Bell Peppers, drained, marinade reserved

Salt and freshly ground black pepper

2 tablespoons minced fresh flat-leaf parsley

SERVES 4

Place the fish in a deep bowl and cover with cold water. Add the garlic cloves and place the bowl in the refrigerator. If you are preparing salt cod, soak for 2 days, changing the water once or twice a day. If you are preparing stockfish, soak it for 4 days, changing the water once or twice a day.

Remove the fish and wash with cold water. It may smell strong. Just wash it well, and soon it will smell sweet. Place the fish and garlic in a medium pot and cover with water. Bring to a boil over medium heat. Boil the fish for about 15 minutes, until it is tender when probed with a fork. Keep the pot uncovered: the boiling water tends to froth up. Drain and allow the fish to cool, about 20 minutes. Discard the garlic. When the fish is cool, use 2 forks to gently shred it into bite-sized pieces.

In the meantime, drop the potatoes into boiling water and cook until they are al dente, about 10 minutes. (If you let the water come up to a boil with the potatoes in it, they will become waterlogged and mealy.) Remove the potatoes, let cool enough to handle, and slice.

In a serving bowl, combine the fish, sliced potatoes, and peppers. The peppers, still in halves, can be sliced into bite-sized pieces ahead of time, but usually I just dump them in and snip them up with scissors to avoid the mess of oily peppers on the counter. Toss the marinade into the salad 1 tablespoon at a time, until the salad is shiny but not oily. Add salt and pepper to taste and garnish with the parsley.

CHICKEN AND SAUSAGES WITH MARINATED RED BELL PEPPERS

In contrast to the usual sausage and peppers dish, here the vinegar in the marinated peppers adds a refreshing, bright acidity. You can prepare this hearty family dish with just chicken or just sausages, but I like a combination. Serve it with sliced boiled potatoes.

2 tablespoons olive oil

4 medium-size sweet Italian sausages, pricked all over with a fork

Salt

4 chicken thighs

1 large onion, chopped (about 2 cups)

Hot red pepper flakes to taste

½ pint Marinated Red Bell Peppers

2 tablespoons chopped flat-leaf parsley

SERVES 4

Heat the oil in a large skillet over medium heat. Add the sausages and start browning them. Salt the chicken thighs and add them to the skillet. Continue browning all the meat, covered (to prevent splattering), until nicely golden, about 30 minutes. If at any point there seems to be a lot of grease, pour it off. After the meat is browned, set it aside and cover with foil to keep warm.

Add the onion to the same pan and sauté over medium heat until translucent, about 5 minutes. Add salt and hot red pepper flakes to taste.

Dump the peppers and marinade into the pan. You will smell the fumes of the vinegar cooking off. You can slice the peppers into bite-sized pieces before throwing them into the pan, but I usually snip them with scissors while in the pan to avoid creating an oily mess on my counters.

Slice the sausage into bite-sized pieces. Once the smell of the vinegar has abated, after about 5 minutes, return the chicken and sausage to the pan. Cook until the meat is heated through, a few minutes. Adjust the seasoning.

Dump onto a serving platter and garnish with parsley.

Lamb and Marinated Red Bell Pepper Stew

The shoulder cut of lamb is inexpensive and usually available at grocery stores. I've made this dish with pork shoulder too, and it is delicious, although it cooks faster. I serve lamb and pepper stew two ways: with soft polenta, rice, boiled cranberry beans, or boiled potatoes; or on warm corn tortillas with chopped red onion and cilantro, and a sliced avocado salad dressed with lime and black pepper on the side. The recipe is adapted from *Saveur* magazine, for which I have written about a zillion stories.

2 pounds sliced bone-in lamb shoulder, cut into large pieces including the bone

2 large garlic cloves, peeled and smashed with flat side of a cook's knife

½ cup dry red or white wine

1 sprig fresh rosemary about 3 inches long

1 tablespoon olive oil, or a little more if needed

1 medium onion, coarsely chopped (about 1 cup)

3 large garlic cloves, coarsely chopped

1 tablespoon sweet paprika (hot is good too)

Salt and freshly ground black pepper to taste

1½ cups homemade or all-natural low-sodium beef or chicken stock, plus more as needed

½ pint Marinated Red Bell Peppers, drained

1 large fresh tomato or ½ cup home-canned (page 163) or canned whole tomatoes, chopped

1 bay leaf

SERVES 4

Place the lamb, smashed garlic cloves, wine, and rosemary in a nonreactive bowl and marinate for 2 hours in the refrigerator, flipping the meat once or twice to be sure the marinade covers all. Drain.

In a medium heavy pot with a tight-fitting lid (2- to 4-quart size), heat the oil over medium-high heat. Brown the meat in the oil in batches, about 5 minutes per side, setting the browned meat aside on a plate as you go (2 batches will do it). It will smell lamby and strong. Don't worry; that goes away. There will be lots of fat. Pour it off and add a bit more oil between batches if necessary.

Return the meat to the pot and add the chopped onion and garlic. Cook until the onion becomes translucent, about 5 minutes. Then add the paprika and salt and pepper to taste. Toss the meat in the spices to coat. Add the stock, peppers, tomato, and bay leaf. Cover and boil gently over medium heat for 1 hour, then partially remove the cover and continue cooking for another hour. Add more stock if the pot gets dry. The consistency should be thick but wet.

Adjust the seasonings and serve.

SAUERKRAUT

There are a lot of little nuances to making sauerkraut. My dad likes to slow-ferment the cabbage directly in quart jars. A Polish friend described cabbage fermented in wooden barrels and dropped into a lake over the winter. For me, I like to see and smell what is going on and be done rather quickly. This recipe, which produces a mild, slightly tangy sauerkraut, is adapted from two different sources: the brilliant *Joy of Pickling* (no home-canning library should be without it) and the recipe recommended by the National Center for Home Food Preservation.

I use the Stonehead variety of cabbage (Savoy, which I prefer to cook with, is too soft). Very fresh cabbage is best, as it will produce the most water during the brining period: I buy it at the farmers' market in August and September. I make sauerkraut in a 1-gallon ceramic crock. Sauerkraut is a dry-salt pickle: the salt pulls liquid out of the cabbage, which creates a brine. The brine protects the cabbage from air while it ferments. Fermenting turns the sugars in the cabbage into acids, which inhibit the growth of spoilers. The sauerkraut is acidic enough to process safely in a water bath for long-term shelf life. (See pages 24 and 17 for more information about pickling and water bath canning.) Canned sauerkraut is good for up to one year.

MAKES 4 PINTS

1½ pounds cabbage (about 1 head)

3 tablespoons pickling salt, plus more as needed

Core and finely shred the cabbage. Combine the cabbage and 1½ tablespoons of the pickling salt in a 1-gallon crock or deep nonreactive bowl. Press the cabbage down with your hands.

Combine 1 quart water and the remaining 1½ tablespoons pickling salt in a bowl and pour into a 1-quart resealable plastic freezer bag. Place the brine-filled bag on top to weigh down the cabbage so the vegetable is below the brine. The cabbage must stay submerged in brine while it ferments. (The brine bag functions as a weight to keep the vegetable submerged and, if the bag leaks, it releases only brine.) Very fresh cabbage will produce enough brine naturally. Older cabbage will need additional brine to cover. (After 24 hours, if your cabbage has not produced enough brine to cover, make up a batch—1 quart of water with

1½ tablespoons of pickling salt dissolved in it—and pour over enough to cover.)

Place the crock in a cool place and allow it to rest for 2 weeks.

Take a look at the sauerkraut every once in a while. You will notice it will bubble and froth a bit. That is good. It will also smell quite strong after a couple of days and then become increasingly mellow.

At the end of 2 weeks, you will notice the fermentation is over—no more bubbling or frothing.

Bring 4 pint jars and their bands to a boil in a large pot of water fitted with a rack. Boil for 10 minutes. Remove the jars with tongs (the tongs don't need to be sterilized). Simmer new lids in a small pan of hot water to soften the rubberized flange. When the jars are dry but still hot, pack the sauerkraut tightly into the jars. Cover with the brine, leaving ½ to ¾ inch of headspace. Wipe the rims, set on the lids, and screw on the bands fingertip tight.

Place the sauerkraut in a pot fitted with a rack and add enough water to cover the jars by 3 inches. Bring the water to a boil over high heat. Process the sauerkraut for 10 minutes. Turn off the heat and remove the top of the pot. After a few minutes, remove the sauerkraut. Don't leave the jars in the water to cool, or the sauerkraut will overprocess.

Allow the jars to cool completely before checking the seals and storing in a cool, dark place for up to a year. Refrigerate after opening.

PENNE WITH SAUERKRAUT

I know this recipe seems bizarre, but it is very tasty. Indeed, it is a typical example of how good a recipe can be when it uses a home-canned food. This is an adaptation of one of my dad's recipes. He can make a pasta dish out of anything.

6 slices bacon (about ¼ pound)

1 pint Sauerkraut

¾ pound penne or other cut pasta such as farfalle

Salt and freshly ground black pepper

½ cup grated Parmesan cheese

¼ cup minced fresh flat-leaf parsley

SERVES 4

Fry the bacon in a medium skillet over medium-high heat until crispy. Drain on paper towels and crumble. Pour out the excess bacon fat. Add the sauerkraut to the skillet and cook over medium-low heat for about 5 minutes, until the sharp smell of the sauerkraut diminishes.

In the meantime, bring a large pot of salted water to boil over high heat. Add the pasta and cook until al dente. Drain. Add the pasta to the sauerkraut. Add salt and pepper to taste. Toss well. Add the reserved bacon crumbles, the Parmesan cheese, and the parsley. Toss and serve immediately.

DUCK WITH SAUERKRAUT

This dish could not be simpler or more delicious. It is adapted from one given to me by my uncle Norfleet of Memphis, Tennessee. Now housebound, he was a passionate duck hunter who belonged to a family club called Claypool's Wild Acres in Arkansas. After a foggy morning of hunting he'd eat a huge southern breakfast at the "clubhouse," a dumpy farmhouse in the middle of rice country, where he'd drink a couple of Bloody Marys made with Clamato, then snore through the entire drive back to town. Later in the day Norfleet would put together a snazzy little dinner, and this was often on the menu.

4 duck legs

2 Pekin duck breasts, halved, or 1 magret breast, cut into 4 pieces

Salt and freshly ground black pepper

1½ pints Sauerkraut

1 cup homemade or all-natural low-sodium chicken stock

2 tablespoons minced fresh flat-leaf parsley

SERVES 4

Preheat the oven to 300°F.

Score the fat on the duck legs and breasts by cutting crosshatches in the fat with the tip of a sharp knife. Season the duck with salt and pepper to taste. Heat a deep ovenproof casserole over high heat. Add the duck pieces fat side down and brown, about 8 minutes. Turn the legs and breasts over and continue cooking until brown, another 4 minutes or so. Add the sauerkraut and stock. Cover and place in the oven.

Bake for 2 hours, until the duck is fork tender. Pour onto a serving platter and garnish with the parsley. Serve promptly.

SAUSAGES WITH SAUERKRAUT

We eat this hearty dish in the winter with a winter vegetable like broccoli rabe sautéed with garlic and hot pepper or Brussels sprouts baked with garlic in a very hot oven until blackened. It all tastes wonderful with a cold beer.

4 small potatoes (I prefer Yukon Gold), peeled

1 tablespoon olive oil

4 medium-size sweet Italian sausages

3 large garlic cloves, minced (about 1½ tablespoons)

1½ pints Sauerkraut

Salt and freshly ground black pepper

½ cup homemade or all-natural low-sodium beef or chicken stock, if needed

Extra virgin olive oil for garnish

3 tablespoons finely chopped fresh flat-leaf parsley

SERVES 4

Bring a medium pot of salted water to a boil over high heat. Add the potatoes and boil for about 10 minutes, until al dente. Drain and cut into bite-sized slices.

Heat the olive oil in a large skillet over a medium heat. Prick the sausages and brown them in the skillet, about 20 minutes. Remove the sausages and cut them into bite-sized slices. (You can also leave the sausages whole, for diners to cut up themselves, a more elegant presentation.)

Place the garlic in the pan you cooked the sausages in and sauté for about 3 minutes, until fragrant. Add the sauerkraut and cook until hot, about 5 minutes, and then add the sausages and potatoes. Add salt to taste. If the dish seems a bit dry, add the stock. Cook for about 5 minutes, covered, until the flavors are well melded.

Pour the sausages, sauerkraut, and potatoes onto a serving platter. Garnish with freshly ground black pepper, a dribble of extra virgin olive oil, and the parsley.

STEWED ONIONS WITH MARJORAM

I grew up eating these onions dumped on top of pasta and garnished with Parmesan cheese, and it's one of my favorites. I also use these onions in omelets and frittatas and in a heap next to a pile of soft scrambled eggs. They make a great bruschetta and make leftover roast meat sandwiches sing.

I like to freeze these onions in pint freezer bags. Freezing can break down the consistency of vegetables, but these onions will be okay, as they are very soft to start with. The only real chore involved in making this dish is slicing all those onions. I peel my onions, cut them into quarters, and slice them in the food processor. This recipe does not call for salt, as salt does not freeze well. It is best to add the seasoning when using the onions in a dish. Stewed onions can stay in the freezer for up to a month, after which the flavor can change. They should be defrosted in the refrigerator. (See page 33 for information on freezing.)

MAKES 6 PINTS

6 tablespoons olive oil

24 medium yellow onions, thinly sliced
(about 24 cups)

9 cups homemade or all-natural
low-sodium beef stock

3 tablespoons dried marjoram

Heat the oil in a large, heavy pot over medium-low heat. Add the onions, and simmer uncovered until very soft, about 30 minutes, stirring every once in a while to ensure they don't burn or stick to the bottom. (The onions will steam if the pot is covered.)

Add the beef stock and marjoram and continue cooking for about 1 hour and 15 minutes. The onions should be light brown and shiny, cooked way down and stewy.

Allow the onions to cool to room temperature and spoon into six 1-pint resealable freezer bags. If you use containers, be sure to leave about 1 inch of headspace, as the onions will expand some as they freeze. Place in the back of the freezer, where it is coldest: 0°F is ideal.

Defrost the onions in the refrigerator. Refrigerate after defrosting and use within a few days.

Stewed Onions with Marjoram Soup

You will need ovenproof soup bowls or large ramekins for this dish.

1 quart homemade or all-natural low-sodium chicken stock

2 pints Stewed Onions with Marjoram, defrosted

Salt and freshly ground black pepper

Four ½-inch-thick slices French or Italian bread, cut to fit the top of your bowls, lightly toasted

2 cups grated Gruyère cheese

4 sprigs fresh marjoram for garnish

SERVES 4

Preheat the oven to 400°F.

Place the stock and stewed onions in a medium pot over medium heat and heat until piping hot. Season with salt and pepper to taste. Place 4 ovenproof bowls on a baking sheet and ladle the soup into the bowls, distributing the onions evenly (I use tongs). Place 1 slice of bread on top of each bowl and then sprinkle ½ cup of grated cheese on top of the bread.

Place on the tray in the oven and heat the soup for about 10 minutes, until the cheese bubbles and browns. The cheese may dribble over the edge of the bowl, which is fine. Garnish with marjoram and serve immediately.

Stewed Onion Quiche

I find tart pans with removable bottoms to be problematic when making tarts with wet batters, as the batter leaks out of cracks in the dough and into the oven. Instead, use a tart pan without a removable bottom or a pie plate.

FOR THE PASTRY

1 cup all-purpose flour, plus more for dusting the board

¼ teaspoon salt

8 tablespoons (1 stick) unsalted butter, very cold

FOR THE FILLING

4 large egg yolks

1 cup heavy cream

Salt and freshly ground black pepper

Pinch of freshly grated nutmeg

1 pint Stewed Onions with Marjoram, defrosted

½ cup Gruyère or Monterey Jack cheese grated on the large holes of a box grater

SERVES 4 AS A MAIN COURSE

To prepare the pastry, combine the flour and salt in a large bowl. Cut in the butter until the mixture has a sandy texture. Work quickly so the butter doesn't get soft. You can also place the flour, salt, and butter in a food processor and pulse. Add 1 tablespoon of cold water and combine, handling the dough as little as possible (or pulsing with the processor). You may need more water to make the dough come together—add it in very small amounts. Do not form into a ball.

Work on a marble countertop or other very smooth surface. Grab a walnut-size piece of the dough (it will be loose and crumbly—it's okay) and smear it with the heel of your hand against the work surface. This process causes the butter to integrate with the flour in long streaks, which will make the pastry nice and flaky. Gather the smear and set aside. Repeat with the remaining dough.

Form the dough chunks into a ball and flatten the ball with the heel of your hand to make a thick patty. Cover with plastic wrap and refrigerate for about 30 minutes.

In the meantime, preheat the oven to 400°F. In a medium bowl, whisk together the egg yolks, heavy cream, salt and pepper to taste, and nutmeg.

Butter a 9-inch tart pan. Roll the chilled pastry on a floured surface, first patting the dough down in all directions by pressing on it with the rolling pin and then rolling out from the middle. Don't roll out the dough any larger than you need to fill the tart pan. Place the pastry into the tart pan.

Spread the onions on the bottom of the tart. Scatter the cheese over the onions. Pour the egg mixture over the cheese and bake for about 25 minutes, until the tart is set.

Allow the quiche to rest for about 10 minutes before serving.

PHEASANT WITH STEWED ONIONS

Pheasant has a tendency to dry out. Braising it in stewed onions is a great way to maintain its moisture. The recipe also works with two split chicken breasts on the bone.

4 strips bacon

4 pheasant breasts, on the bone (about 2 pounds)

2 tablespoons olive oil

4 garlic cloves with skins

4 tablespoons Cognac

Salt and freshly ground black pepper

6 cups Stewed Onions with Marjoram, defrosted

1 cup chicken or duck stock, or water

SERVES 4

Preheat the oven to 350°F.

Wrap 1 strip of bacon around each pheasant breast. Tie the bacon strip to the breast with a piece of culinary string.

Heat the oil in an ovenproof heavy-bottomed skillet with a fitted top or a Dutch oven over medium heat. Add the pheasant and the garlic cloves and brown on both sides, about 5 minutes per side. Add the Cognac and turn up the heat to high. Cook the birds until the Cognac evaporates, a couple of minutes. Season the birds with salt and pepper, and add the onions and stock. Cover the pot and place it in the oven. Cook the birds for 15 to 20 minutes, turning them periodically. Add a little more stock if the pan looks dry.

SUCCOTASH

Pressure canning corn—the only way you can preserve it in a jar—is a great way to retain that super-sweet taste of summer. No frozen commercial product compares—even home-frozen corn doesn't retain as much sweetness as pressure canned. However, the sugar in sweet corn causes it to brown during canning. (You won't have a discoloration problem with starchy corn.) Discoloration does not hurt the food, but it is disappointing to see that bright yellow color disappear. This recipe is adapted from *Stocking Up,* an excellent resource.

Pressure canning brings the food to a high enough heat to ensure all bacteria are killed. (See page 28 for information on pressure canning and read the instructions for your particular pressure canner.) Stored in a cool, dark place, the succotash is good for up to a year.

MAKES 5 PINTS

10 ears sweet corn, husked

¾ pound fresh lima or other shell beans (about 2½ cups shelled)

2½ teaspoons salt

Bring a large pot of water to a boil over high heat and add the corn. Cook for about 4 minutes, until the corn is tender. Drain the corn and allow it to cool enough to handle. Cut the kernels off the corn. Do not cut so close to the cob that you "milk" it. You should have about 5 cups of kernels.

In a large bowl, combine the corn and beans.

Place ½ teaspoon of salt in the bottom of each of 5 scalded pint jars. (To scald, simply dip the jars in boiling water. You don't need to sterilize the jars, as you will be processing them for over 10 minutes.)

Simmer new lids in a small pan of hot water to soften the rubberized flange. Fill the jars, leaving 1 inch of headspace. Wipe the rims, set on the lids, and screw on the bands fingertip tight.

Place the rack in the bottom of your pressure canner. Add 2 to 3 inches of boiling water, and place the jars on the rack. Align the cover handles so they are locked into position as per the instructions for your pressure canner. Remove the pressure regulator from the steam vent. Heat the canner over high heat. Allow steam to be released from the vent for 7 to 10 minutes and then put the pressure regulator over the steam vent. Watch the pressure regulator. When it is about to reach 10 pounds of pressure, lower the heat slightly so that once it reaches 10 pounds, it stays there. Check periodically to ensure the pressure stays at 10 pounds. Usually, once you've got the heat right, the pressure will

become stable. If you are a little over, it's okay. Just don't go under 10 pounds. If the pressure dips under 10 pounds, you can't count those minutes against the hour you must process the corn. First bring the canner back up to pressure by increasing the heat and then continue timing. Process the jars at 10 pounds of pressure for 1 hour.

Turn off the heat and allow the pressure to drop naturally. When the canner is depressurized (this will be evident as per the instructions for your specific pressure canner), remove the gauge, then the top. Remove the jars and allow them to rest for at least 6 hours. Check the seals and store in a cool, dark place for up to a year.

NOTE The only failures I have had in pressure canning succotash occurred when I overfilled the jars, so be sure to leave 1 inch of headspace.

SUCCOTASH GRATIN

This side dish is very sweet and rich. We ladle it alongside plain grilled meats and like to have a green salad as well, to balance out the creaminess of the gratin. Succotash gratin also makes a nice first course with a few grilled sea scallops served on top. For a more elegant presentation, cook the gratin in four individual ramekins set on a baking sheet.

1 pint Succotash

½ cup heavy cream

⅓ cup plus ¼ cup Gruyère cheese, grated on the large holes of a box grater

¼ teaspoon freshly grated nutmeg

Salt and freshly ground black pepper

SERVES 4

Preheat the oven to 350°F.

Combine the succotash and the cream in a small saucepan and heat over medium heat for 3 to 5 minutes, until it is bubbling. Add ⅓ cup of the cheese and take the pot off the heat. Stir to combine. Add the nutmeg and salt and pepper to taste.

Dump the gratin into a small, deep ovenproof casserole dish. Sprinkle the remaining ¼ cup of Gruyère on top and bake, uncovered, for 30 minutes, until the cheese begins to brown. Serve immediately.

< FRIED POBLANO CHILES STUFFED WITH SUCCOTASH

FRIED POBLANO CHILES STUFFED WITH SUCCOTASH

This recipe is time consuming but very worthwhile, if only as a means of mastering the fried poblano. You can stuff anything into a poblano and fry it and it will taste good. People just go crazy for them—kids, gourmands, grandmas—and having the succotash on hand makes the job that much easier. I serve these as a side course, with sour cream, but they make a great vegetarian entrée too. I prefer to use mild poblanos, which are the more common in markets. Sometimes you can smell a hot poblano when you buy it, but usually it's when you are removing the seedpod that it becomes obvious which peppers have the heat. I just separate those out for the capsaicin junkies.

1 cup all-purpose flour

1 teaspoon baking powder

Salt and freshly ground black pepper

1¼ cups lager beer

8 mild poblano chiles

½ pound Monterey Jack cheese, cut into 8 sticks about 3 inches long

1 tablespoon unsalted butter

½ medium onion, chopped (about ½ cup)

2 garlic cloves, minced (about 1 tablespoon)

1 pint Succotash

Vegetable oil (not olive oil—it's too heavy) for frying

4 tablespoons sour cream for garnish

4 lime wedges for garnish

SERVES 4

Preheat the broiler.

Make the batter by combining the flour, baking powder, a pinch of salt, and the beer in a medium bowl. The batter should be the consistency of runny yogurt. Refrigerate the batter for about 1 hour.

In the meantime, place the chiles on a baking sheet and broil them until the skin blisters, about 2 minutes. Turn the chiles often so they char all over. Remove the chiles, and as soon as you can handle them, slip off the skins. (You can also place them in a paper bag for a few minutes. This makes removal of the skin easier, but it steam-cooks the flesh a bit, making the chiles more delicate and difficult to handle during the stuffing stage.) Remove the seedpod by cutting around the stem and pulling out the pod whole. Gently pull out the veins. Insert a stick of cheese into each chile.

Heat the butter in a medium pan over medium heat. Add the onion and garlic and cook until the onion is translucent, about 5 minutes. Stir in the succotash and season with salt and pepper to taste.

Spoon the succotash into the chiles and close the chiles up with a toothpick.

Heat 1½ inches of vegetable oil in a large nonstick skillet over medium heat until hot. (You can test the hotness of the oil by throwing in a pinch of flour. If it pops, the oil is ready.) Remove the batter from the refrigerator. The batter will have puffed up some; this is good. Dip the chiles in the batter. I use my fingers. If some of the succotash rolls out, don't worry, because once the batter starts to fry it will seal the chiles up. Place the chiles in the hot oil, as many as will fit roomily in the skillet at a time (I usually can fit 3 to 4). Fry the chiles until golden, about 1 minute per side. Drain the chiles on paper towels. Allow the oil to heat up again before adding more chiles, because if the oil is too cool, your chiles will be greasy (they'll still taste good).

Serve with sour cream and lime wedges.

NOTE Believe it or not, these chiles can be reheated and eaten the next day. They won't be as crisp, but they'll be delicious. I just warm them up in the toaster oven.

Succotash with Rice

This is basically a marinara sauce combined with rice and succotash. It is a very hearty dish, surprisingly tasty, which we tend to eat in a bowl like soup, with a salad and a glass of red wine—I like a Spanish Rioja, made from the Tempranillo grape. (There are three subzones of Rioja: Alta, Alavesa, and Baja. All three regions produce wines that are wonderful with this dish; the wines from Alta are the most delicate, those from Baja the biggest.)

2 slices bacon, coarsely chopped

1 medium onion, minced (about 1 cup)

2 medium carrots, minced (about 1 cup)

1 garlic clove, minced (about 1 teaspoon)

2 cups chopped fresh tomatoes, or canned whole tomatoes (without puree)

1 tablespoon minced fresh basil

1 teaspoon dried oregano

1 tablespoon unsalted butter

Salt and freshly ground black pepper

½ cup basmati rice

1 cup homemade or all-natural low-sodium chicken stock

1 pint Succotash

⅓ cup grated Parmesan

2 tablespoons minced fresh flat-leaf parsley

SERVES 4

Fry the bacon in a deep saucepan over medium-high heat until the fat is rendered and the meat is just crispy, about 5 minutes. Remove the bacon to a paper towel to drain. Add the onion, carrots, and garlic to the pan and cook until the vegetables are soft, about 7 minutes. Add the tomatoes and cover. Turn the heat down to medium and cook for 15 minutes, until the tomatoes have disintegrated. Turn off the heat. Either puree the sauce in the pot with an immersion blender or pass the sauce through a food mill and return it to the pot. Add the bacon, basil, oregano, butter, and salt and pepper to taste.

In the meantime, place the rice and stock in a small saucepan and bring to a boil over medium heat. Turn the heat down to a simmer, cover, and cook until the rice is tender, 15 to 20 minutes. Remove from the heat and let sit, covered, for 5 minutes.

Add the succotash and rice to the sauce and heat through. Garnish with the grated Parmesan and parsley. Serve hot.

TOMATOES

There is probably no more common or more satisfying food to put up than tomatoes. Home-canned tomatoes are superior in every way to any commercially canned product, regardless of provenance. Prepared when the tomatoes are in season in the late summer, they are inexpensive to preserve, shelf stable, and, when used in recipes, produce significantly better dishes. If I could put up only one food, it would be tomatoes.

Selecting tomatoes to can is easy but important. Though tomatoes are a fruit, they are usually pH 4.5 or 4.6, which is right on the borderline of foods you can safely process in a water bath. Different circumstances can vary the acidity (pH) of tomatoes just

enough to tip tomatoes into the iffy category, where you either have to acidify them by adding citric acid or lemon juice or can them in a pressure canner versus a water bath. These circumstances are decay and damage caused by insects, age, and manhandling; tomatoes ripened in the shade or off the vine; and tomatoes that have been exposed to a frost. There is also some variability within species. Anecdotally, my friend Linda Long, a very fine Colorado canner and a real western lady, told me that early-ripening tomatoes should be avoided. "I don't can any tomato that is ripe before September," she says. Given the choice between globe and plum tomatoes, choose plum tomatoes: they are more acidic. Do not refrigerate tomatoes you intend to can, as refrigeration undermines the flavor. These days the Feds are recommending you acidify all tomato products, and considering the pH variability in different tomatoes, this makes sense. You can use 2 tablespoons of lemon juice per pint, but I call for ¼ teaspoon of citric acid because I find it simpler. If you use lemon juice, use bottled, as commercial products have a consistent pH and fresh lemons can vary in acidity.

I can tomatoes two ways. While the following recipe is for my grade A canned tomatoes, with skin and seeds removed and the tomatoes crushed, I also raw pack: I shove halved tomatoes into the jars, add the citric acid and salt, and process. Raw pack is incredibly simple. There are two downsides, however. You have to process raw tomatoes for about 10 minutes longer than tomatoes that are preheated in the pan (you also have to process them longer because it takes the heat longer to penetrate and come to temperature in half a tomato than the same volume of crushed tomato). The other caveat is when it comes time to cook the tomatoes in a recipe, you will want to remove those skins and seeds by pushing the tomatoes through a food mill anyway. Tomato skins tend to curl in the sauce and stick to the top of your mouth when you eat them, and the seeds are bitter. If you do cook recipes with tomatoes and leave the skins and seeds on, choose recipes that call for short (30 minutes or less) cooking times. That's because the longer you cook a tomato with the skins and seeds, the more bitter it will become.

Sometimes I remove my tomatoes from the canner to find the pulp has separated from the juice. This is caused by an enzyme in the tomato that becomes activated when the tomato is exposed to air, either by skinning and/or cutting and crushing. The enzyme breaks down pectin, causing the solids and liquids to separate. The sooner those skinned, cut, or crushed tomatoes hit the heat, the better, as heat stops the enzymatic action. (This is also why you almost always blanch foods before freezing them.) When this happens, I just flip over the jars and let them cool upside down. This usually remixes the pulp and liquids. But if it doesn't, it's okay: the tomatoes are still good to eat.

I add salt for flavor, but you don't have to. I also sometimes add a fresh basil leaf to my raw pack tomatoes. I have yet to discover whether adding a basil leaf constitutes a safety hazard, but generations of family on my dad's side have been putting up tomatoes with basil, so I do too. You could put in dried oregano if you like. Since the herb is dehydrated, making it an uninhabitable environment for bacteria, there is no fear of spoilers hitching a ride into your jars.

I have had only two tomato canning failures in twelve years of canning them—and I can lots and lots. Once I heard this wicked fizzing in the cupboard, and when I opened it I could smell something rotten, like the way the inside of a vase smells after the flowers have died. It took about two seconds to locate the jar, which I opened and flushed. Another time, I produced an entire bad case. The jars seemed sealed when I finished processing them, and I left them in my cabin over the winter, to enjoy when I next returned. At some point the seals loosened, to the point where I could easily pull them off with my fingers. You should not eat tomatoes that have been stored on the shelf with anything less than a super-tight seal.

CANNED TOMATOES

I like to use wide-mouth jars for tomatoes (actually, for everything), as they are easier to pack. (See page 17 for more information about water bath canning.)

MAKES 6 PINTS

6 to 8 pounds ripe unblemished tomatoes, unrefrigerated

6 teaspoons salt

1½ teaspoons citric acid

Bring a large pot of water to a boil over high heat. Drop the tomatoes into the boiling water, count off 10 seconds, and then remove.

With a sharp paring knife, slit the tomato skins and peel them off. They will come off easily. Core the tomatoes and tear them in half, squeezing out the seeds. Toss into a pot. I drop the skins and seeds into a colander over a bowl. A lot of tomato juice is saved this way, which you can add to your canning tomatoes or refrigerate for use in, oh, say, Bloody Marys.

Crush the tomatoes. You can use a food processor or a potato masher. I squeeze the tomatoes with my hands because I am lazy and don't want the additional cleanup. A few chunks are okay.

Heat the tomatoes and boil gently for 5 minutes. The tomatoes may get a bit foamy on top. It's okay.

Have ready 6 scalded pint jars and their bands.

(To scald, simply dip the jars in boiling water. You don't need to sterilize the jars, as you will be processing them for over 10 minutes.) Simmer new lids in a small pan of hot water, to soften the rubberized flange. Dump 1 teaspoon of salt and ¼ teaspoon citric acid into each jar. Ladle in the hot tomatoes, leaving ½ to ¾ inch of headspace. Wipe the rims, set on the lids, and screw on the bands fingertip tight.

Place the jars in a pot fitted with a rack and add enough water to cover the jars by 3 inches. Bring the water to a boil over high heat. The tomatoes process for a long time, which is a problem, since water can splash out during the boil. If the tops of the jars are not covered with water at any point, you have to delete the time that the cans were not totally submerged, add water, bring back to a boil, and begin timing again, deducting any time in which the jars were not submerged. Process the tomatoes for 40 minutes, then turn off the heat. Wait 5 minutes or so, then remove the jars and let them rest. If some pulp fizzes out of the jars, don't panic: they will probably still seal. After about 8 hours, remove the bands and check the lids. If the seals are tight, label the jars and store them in a cool, dark place for up to a year. You do not need to store the jars with the screw top on. The lid is enough.

Ed Giobbi's Sweet Marinara Sauce

I publish this recipe of my dad's in all my books because it is a good, simple recipe that everyone adores. It produces an elegant, sweet sauce that you can use in any recipe that calls for marinara sauce. The sauce freezes well, but don't add the salt and pepper if you plan to freeze. Just pour the hot sauce into a food-grade plastic container and refrigerate. When it is cold, place in the freezer. The sauce will hold for 4 to 6 months.

1 tablespoon olive oil

1 medium onion, chopped (about 1 cup)

2 medium carrots, chopped (about 1 cup)

2 large garlic cloves, chopped (about 1 tablespoon)

2 pints Canned Tomatoes

1 tablespoon chopped fresh basil

1 teaspoon dried oregano

Salt and freshly ground black pepper

2 tablespoons unsalted butter

MAKES 4 CUPS

Heat the oil in a large saucepan over medium heat. Add the onion, carrots, and garlic. Cook until the vegetables are soft, about 10 minutes. Add the tomatoes and cook for 15 minutes, until the sauce is bubbling. Do not boil it hard. Turn down the heat if you have to.

Push the hot sauce through a food mill for a very smooth sauce or, if you have one of these nifty things, puree the vegetables with an immersion blender.

Return the sauce to the heat, add the herbs and salt and pepper to taste and cook for another 15 minutes, until you can smell the herbs perfuming the sauce. Add the butter, stir it in until it is melted, and serve.

NOTE You can add 1/2 cup half-and-half or heavy cream to make this into a pink sauce. It will look curdled at first, but don't worry. Once you toss the sauce with pasta, the starch from the pasta will bind the sauce and it will become silky again.

SMOOTH TOMATO SOUP

My kids love grilled cheese sandwiches with tomato soup. We always have all the fixings for this fast comfort meal. And it is always good.

2 pints Canned Tomatoes

½ cup half-and-half

1 handful large cut pasta, like rigatoni

2 tablespoons minced fresh basil

Salt and freshly ground black pepper

SERVES 4

Pass the tomatoes through a food mill to remove any residual skins or seeds. Be sure the tomatoes are smooth: chunks can be acidic in this dish. Heat the tomatoes in a large saucepan over medium-low heat. Bring to a gentle boil. Add the cream. Allow the cream to heat through, about 4 minutes. It will look curdled. It's okay. Add the pasta and stir just until the sauce is smooth again. You aren't cooking the pasta to eat—just adding it long enough to allow some of its starch to be released into the soup. The starch from the pasta helps bind the cream and tomatoes. Remove the pasta with a slotted spoon and discard. Add the basil and salt and pepper to taste. Stir and serve.

NOTE For a variation, add 1 cup cooked sweet corn instead of the pasta . . . and then leave it in.

STEWED BEEF WITH TOMATOES AND GARLIC

This incredibly tasty dish is prepared in many Mediterranean countries. My Italian grandmother made a version, though with lesser cuts of meat. You can stake out your own particular version by adding fresh herbs or spices. The tomatoes, which are acidic, tenderize the beef as well as throwing off lots of great flavor.

2 pounds beef round roast

2 pints Canned Tomatoes

1 medium head of garlic, cloves separated and peeled (not elephant garlic)

2 tablespoons olive oil

Salt and freshly ground black pepper

SERVES 4

Preheat the oven to 325°F.

Combine the meat, tomatoes, garlic, oil, and salt and pepper to taste in a deep, heavy pot with a tight-fitting lid. Bake for about 4 hours, until the beef is meltingly tender, stirring occasionally.

We like to serve the beef on tortillas, but it's great with rice or boiled potatoes, too.

ZUCCHINI FLOWER SAUCE

There was a time when I could get zucchini flowers only by plundering my dad's garden. But this delicious flower has hit the mainstream, and I can now purchase huge, fresh specimens at the farmers' market all summer long.

I love the delicate taste of zucchini flowers. I batter them, sometimes stuff them, and fry them to serve as an appetizer. But the season always seems to end too soon. What a joy to find that zucchini flower sauce freezes beautifully, so I can enjoy them in December! The sauce holds for three months in the freezer. (See page 33 for information on freezing.)

MAKES 4 CUPS

1 pound zucchini flowers

3 tablespoons olive oil

1 medium onion, finely chopped (about 1 cup)

4 cups homemade or all-natural low-sodium chicken stock

½ teaspoon saffron threads, soaked in 1 tablespoon warm water for a few minutes

2 tablespoons unsalted butter

Check the insides of the zucchini flowers for insects. Unless you think the plants were sprayed with insecticides, do not wash. Coarsely chop.

Heat the oil in a large skillet over medium heat. Add the onion and sauté until translucent, about 5 minutes. Add the chopped zucchini flowers and sauté over medium-low heat for about 5 minutes, until the flowers are soft. You will smell their delicate perfume.

Heat the stock to a simmer over low heat. Add the saffron with its water. Pour the saffron-flavored stock over the flowers and simmer gently over low heat for 15 to 20 minutes, until the stock reduces by about a quarter. Do not add salt or pepper unless you are going to serve immediately.

Spoon the sauce into four 1-cup freezer containers (do not reuse old deli containers, which aren't necessarily food grade), leaving ½ inch of headspace for expansion. Immediately place in the freezer, preferably in the back, where it is coldest. The quicker the sauce freezes, the better the texture will be when you defrost. The sauce will keep for 3 months.

Defrost the sauce in the refrigerator for about 4 hours or, to speed up defrosting, place the closed container in a bowl of cool water for about 2 hours.

Zucchini Flower Risotto

This is a terrific first course because it suits so many menus. I love it before fish, but I've also served it before entrées of grilled meat and braised chicken. As a light dinner followed by a salad and a piece of fruit, this risotto is perfect. You can also serve the sauce on spaghettini cooked in chicken stock and garnished with freshly ground black pepper.

To my taste, the best risotto is loose, served in a shallow bowl, and eaten with a spoon.

1 tablespoon olive oil

1 large shallot, minced (about 2 tablespoons)

1 cup riso Carnaroli or Arborio rice

½ cup dry white wine

1 quart homemade or all-natural low-sodium chicken stock, warmed

1 cup defrosted Zucchini Flower Sauce

Salt and freshly ground black pepper

⅓ cup grated Parmesan cheese

1 teaspoon grated lemon zest

2 tablespoons minced fresh flat-leaf parsley

SERVES 4

Heat the oil in a medium heavy pot over medium heat. Add the shallot and cook for about 1 minute, until soft and fragrant. Add the rice and stir to coat with the oil and shallot, about 1 minute. The rice will take on a translucent quality. Add the wine—it will boil up, then settle down—and cook until the wine is absorbed, about 2 minutes. Add 1 cup of the warm stock, stir, and cook until the rice absorbs most of the stock, about 5 minutes. You don't have to sit over risotto, stirring and stirring, unless the quality of the rice is poor or it is old. (See page 84 for more information about risotto rice.)

Keep adding the stock 1 cup at a time, allowing the rice to absorb most of the stock before adding more, stirring often. Do not allow the risotto and stock to boil: it is best to keep the heat at medium-low and the risotto simmering gently. Do be sure the rice is always wet. If so, your risotto won't stick. If it does stick, it is because the rice is cooking in too little liquid.

In the meantime, warm the zucchini flower sauce in a small pan over medium-low heat.

When the rice is almost al dente, add the zucchini flower sauce. Stir in the sauce and continue cooking for about 3 minutes. If you jiggle the pot, the risotto should undulate.

Take the risotto off the heat and add salt and pepper to taste. Stir in the Parmesan cheese and lemon zest. Garnish with parsley and freshly ground black pepper.

The longer the risotto rests, the firmer it will become. Resting will not affect the flavor, but it will affect the texture, so for best results, serve immediately.

ZUCCHINI FLOWER QUESADILLAS

I am not a quesadilla fan in general, but these are quite elegant. I like to serve them with a soft sliced avocado dressed with minced cilantro and a bit of extra virgin olive oil. I avoid salting this dish—enough seems to come off the cheese and chicken stock in the frozen sauce.

Olive oil

4 large flour tortillas

1½ cups grated Monterey Jack cheese

About ¾ cup defrosted Zucchini Flower Sauce

Freshly ground black pepper

SERVES 4

Heat a skillet large enough to hold a tortilla over medium-low heat. Rub a small amount of olive oil—about ½ teaspoon—in the bottom of the skillet. Lay 1 tortilla in the skillet. Flip the tortilla over a few times, until it is lightly browned and puffed with air pockets. Then sprinkle a quarter of the cheese over it, followed by 3 tablespoons of the zucchini flower sauce and a few grinds of black pepper. Cover the skillet. After a minute the cheese should be melted. Remove the cover and flip half of the tortilla over, as you would an omelet. Remove from the skillet, cut into wedges, and repeat for the remaining tortillas. Serve immediately.

SOLE WITH ZUCCHINI FLOWER SAUCE

Sole is such a fragile, delicate fish that I avoid cooking it with too many flavors. But zucchini flower sauce, which is as much about perfume as anything else, is a perfect foil. I use Dover sole when I can get it, though flounder will do. Serve this dish with boiled potatoes tossed in herb butter.

1 tablespoon olive oil

4 Dover sole fillets (about 1 pound)

Salt and freshly ground black pepper

1 cup defrosted Zucchini Flower Sauce

2 tablespoons minced fresh flat-leaf parsley

SERVES 4

Place the oven rack 6 to 8 inches from the broiler and preheat the broiler.

Lightly oil a baking sheet. Place the sole on the sheet and add a few grinds of black pepper. I do not salt the sole, especially if I am not going to pop it under the broiler promptly, because the tender flesh of the fish is easily overwhelmed by salt. Place the fish under the broiler and broil for about 5 minutes, until the flesh is white and separates easily when prodded with the tines of a fork. (Very thin fillets will take less time; flounder fillets will take a few minutes longer.)

In the meantime, heat the zucchini flower sauce in a small saucepan over medium-low heat until it is simmering hot, a couple of minutes. Add salt to taste.

Spoon the sauce over the cooked fish. Garnish with parsley and freshly ground black pepper and serve immediately.

BEANS, NUTS, AND FUNGI

FAVA BEAN CREAM

Fresh fava beans—broad beans—have a short, glorious season in the spring, though I have seen them in late summer too. They are time consuming to prepare for cooking, as you have to remove both the pod and the skin, but it's worthwhile. I like to preserve what the Italians call the *crema di fava,* a highly versatile and tasty puree. Besides the recipes given here, I love to loosen the fava bean cream with a little extra virgin olive oil and serve it in a puddle under broiled scallops or smear a tablespoon on bruschetta. Sometimes I make thin spaghetti with oil and garlic and toss in a few tablespoons of Fava Bean Cream to dress it up. I highly recommend you fool around with the quantities of the ingredients to suit your taste in the base recipe, which does not call for salt because salt does not freeze well; add the salt when you use the cream in a recipe. Fava bean cream can stay frozen for up to 6 months. (See page 33 for information about freezing.)

MAKES 3 CUPS

8 pounds fava beans in the pod (see Note)

1 cup homemade or all-natural low-sodium chicken stock, warmed

6 garlic cloves, smashed with the flat side of a cook's knife

6 tablespoons pine nuts

3 tablespoons fresh lemon juice

Shell the fava beans; you should have about 3 pounds shelled.

Bring a large pot of water to a boil over high heat. Dump in the fava beans and cook until al dente, 3 to 5 minutes. Drain and rinse the beans in cold water. (You can refrigerate the beans for 24 hours before continuing if you like.) To remove the skins, pinch a half-moon of skin off one end of the bean with your thumbnail and squeeze out the flesh. You will end up with about 2 pounds of fava bean flesh.

In a food processor, combine the fava beans, stock, garlic, pine nuts, and lemon juice. Process into a loose paste.

Have ready two 1-cup freezer containers and two ½-cup freezer containers with tight-fitting lids that have been washed well in very hot soapy water and dried. (I use Tupperware.)

Pour the hot sauce into the freezer containers, leaving ½ inch of headspace for expansion. Put on the lids, date the containers, and place in the refrigerator. When cool, transfer the fava bean cream to the freezer.

< CREAM OF FAVA SOUP

The sauce is good for up to 6 months. You can heat the sauce without thawing, but you may need to place the container in a bowl of water for a few minutes to make it easier to dump into the pan.

NOTE When choosing fresh fava beans, avoid pods bulging with fat beans. This indicates maturity and will lead to a starchier end product.

CREAM OF FAVA SOUP

This is a ladylike soup, very fine and tasty. Once I served it in fragile, antique bone china consommé cups that I inherited from my great-grandmother, and the gals I had over for lunch loved it. The higher the grade of stock you use, the better this dish will turn out. Homemade is the best, but stocks made by delis and specialty markets can be good, too.

2 cups Fava Bean Cream

2 cups homemade or all-natural low-sodium chicken stock

4 slices baguette, cut into 1/2-inch cubes

2 teaspoons extra virgin olive oil

Salt and freshly ground black pepper to taste

1/4 cup heavy cream

4 scant tablespoons crème fraîche or sour cream (optional)

SERVES 4

Preheat the broiler.

Combine the fava bean cream and the stock in a medium pot and warm over medium heat, stirring occasionally. Just as the soup begins to boil, take it off the heat and let it come to room temperature. (For a very luxurious soup, pass the fava bean cream and stock through a China cap or very fine sieve.)

In the meantime, scatter the bread cubes on a baking sheet and broil until browned all over, shaking the pan to turn the croutons, about 1 minute. (For the record, I am a chronic toast burner. The only way I can avoid burning the croutons is if I keep the oven door open, so I can see and smell what's going on.) Remove the croutons, dribble olive oil and salt over them, and toss.

Add the heavy cream and salt and pepper to taste to the fava soup. Serve garnished with the croutons and a little crème fraîche if you like. I like this soup best at room temperature, but it chills nicely. Refrigerate the soup in a pitcher (without the croutons or crème fraîche) for about 90 minutes. Add the garnishes right before serving.

Risotto with Fava Bean Cream

For preparing risotto, Arborio rice will do, but I prefer riso Carnaroli, which the chef at Felidia in New York calls "the king of rice." The grains do not overcook as easily, and the individual grains retain their integrity. The rice has a lovely perfume that indicates its freshness: the shelf life of these grains is 18 months, and the better products are dated. Old rice cannot retain an al dente state: it quickly becomes mushy.

2 tablespoons olive oil

1½ cups minced onion (1 large onion)

1½ cups riso Carnaroli or Arborio rice

¾ cup dry white wine

½ cup Fava Bean Cream

3 cups homemade or all-natural low-sodium chicken stock, warmed

Salt and freshly ground black pepper

3 tablespoons minced fresh chives or basil

2 tablespoons grated Parmesan cheese

SERVES 4

Heat the oil in a heavy pot over medium heat. (A wide shallow pot will cook risotto faster and more evenly than a small deep one.) Add the onion and cook until wilted, about 5 minutes. Add the rice and stir until it is well coated with oil. The rice will become slightly translucent, and the grains will individuate; this is good. Add the white wine (it will boil up rapidly for a moment) and cook over medium-low heat until the wine is absorbed, about 5 minutes. The rice may stick, so stir often, though you don't have to stir it constantly if you keep the rice wet. Add 2 tablespoons of the fava bean cream. Cook until the rice absorbs the cream, a couple of minutes, then add the first cup of stock. Stir periodically, allowing the rice to absorb the stock and ensuring the rice doesn't stick to the bottom of the pot, about 5 minutes. Add the next cup of stock, and so on, until you have used all the stock. Test the rice for doneness by sampling a grain. It should be yielding but firm to the bite, and the texture of the overall dish should be as soft as porridge.

Add the remaining fava bean cream and salt and pepper to taste and cook for another couple of minutes, stirring the cream through the rice. Turn off the heat and allow the rice to rest for a few minutes. The rice will continue to absorb the fava bean cream.

Serve the risotto in shallow bowls, garnished with a sprinkle of fresh chives and grated Parmesan. You can also dribble a little extra virgin olive oil over the dish if you like.

STEWED SWORDFISH WITH FAVA BEAN CREAM

This dish is an adaptation of one my father, Edward Giobbi, created for our book, *Italian Family Dining*. He made it with peas and stock, and I couldn't have imagined a simpler dish until I started using my frozen fava bean cream. The fish is excellent served atop a large piece of bruschetta.

5 tablespoons olive oil

1 medium onion, thinly sliced

3 garlic cloves, thinly sliced

Hot red pepper flakes

2 tablespoons white wine vinegar

2 tablespoons chopped fresh flat-leaf parsley

½ cup Fava Bean Cream

¼ to ½ cup homemade or all-natural low-sodium fish or chicken stock, warmed, or warm water

Salt and freshly ground black pepper

1¼ pounds swordfish, cut into 3-inch pieces

2 tablespoons chopped fresh mint or parsley (optional)

SERVES 4

Heat 3 tablespoons of the olive oil in a medium pan over medium heat. Add the onion, garlic, and hot red pepper flakes to taste. Cook until the onion is wilted, about 5 minutes. Add the vinegar and parsley, lower the heat to medium-low, and cook until the vinegar evaporates, about 2 minutes. Add the fava bean cream and enough stock to create a loose sauce, about the consistency of milk. Stir to combine. Cook until the sauce boils, then take it off the heat. Add salt and pepper to taste.

In a large skillet, heat the remaining 2 tablespoons of olive oil over medium heat. Season the fish and sauté it in the oil until it is golden on both sides, about 5 minutes total.

Dump the fava and onion sauce into the skillet with the fish and combine gently. Garnish with fresh mint if you like and serve immediately.

FORIANA SAUCE

Foriana sauce comes from the island of Ischia off the coast of Naples, where it is served on pasta as a Lenten dish. This is my father's recipe, one I often serve to vegetarians, who almost always have an epiphany when they taste it on spaghetti. It makes a quick and exotic bruschetta topping or stuffing for broiled clams, and indeed, when added to other dishes, Foriana sauce adds a Moorish quality that is savory, sweet, and spicy. The sauce is heated, then packed in sterilized jars, covered with olive oil, and refrigerated. The oil acts as a barrier between the sauce and spoilers in the air in the fridge, and refrigeration retards the growth of spoilers. (See page 37 for more information on preserving in oil.) Foriana sauce lasts about 10 days.

MAKES 3 HALF-PINTS

1 cup walnuts

1 cup pine nuts

5 tablespoons sliced garlic (about 10 large cloves)

1 tablespoon dried oregano

3 tablespoons high-quality Italian olive oil, plus more for covering the jars

½ cup golden raisins

Salt and freshly ground black pepper

Place the walnuts, pine nuts, and garlic in a food processor and pulse until the nuts resemble damp granola. Add the oregano and pulse a few more times to combine.

Heat the olive oil in a medium skillet over medium heat. Add the nut mixture, the raisins, and salt and pepper to taste. Cook for about 5 minutes, stirring constantly to avoid burning.

Bring 3 half-pint jars and their bands to a boil in a large pot of water fitted with a rack. Boil for 10 minutes. Remove the jars with tongs (the tongs don't need to be sterilized). Simmer new lids in a small pan of hot water to soften the rubberized flange. When the jars are dry but still hot, pack in the Foriana sauce, eliminating as many air pockets as you can. (I press down with the knuckles of my index and middle fingers to pack the sauce—be sure your hands are clean.) Fill the jars to about 1 inch below the rim. Add a ½-inch layer of oil to cover. Wipe the rims with a paper towel, set on the lids, screw on the bands, and refrigerate. Check on the sauce a day after you make it: you may need to add more oil to ensure it is completely covered.

Be sure to cover the surface of the Foriana sauce

with oil after each use. Pour or spoon off the oil and remove only the quantity of sauce that you need for a dish and allow that to come to room temperature.

Cover the remaining sauce in the jar with fresh oil and return it to the fridge promptly.

Brodetto Foriana

Brodetto is a fish stew from the Adriatic coast of Italy. The invention of fishermen's wives, it is traditionally made with the small, bony fish that don't always sell. Although I have never seen a Foriana version (the base recipe is one my father makes often), such an adaptation is true to the spirit of this enduring but ever-changing dish. You can substitute any fish: just avoid delicate ones like sole, which fall apart when braised. If you use squid, which is an excellent choice, cut it into rings and sauté it gently in oil for 10 minutes before adding it to the stew.

2 tablespoons olive oil

1 medium onion, finely chopped (about 1 cup)

½ green bell pepper, finely chopped (about 1 cup)

2 garlic cloves, finely chopped (about 1 tablespoon)

2 tablespoons finely chopped fresh flat-leaf parsley

Hot red pepper flakes

¼ cup white wine vinegar

2 cups coarsely chopped fresh or canned whole tomatoes

Salt

Two 6-inch monkfish fillets or other dense white fish like bass or halibut, cut into 4 pieces each

8 littleneck clams or mussels or a combination

4 large scallops

4 large shrimp, peeled and deveined

6 tablespoons Foriana Sauce

4 large pieces toasted Italian bread

SERVES 4

Heat the oil in a large saucepan over medium heat. Add the onion, green pepper, garlic, parsley, and hot red pepper flakes to taste. Sauté for about 5 minutes, until the vegetables are soft. Add the vinegar and cook for a few seconds, until it evaporates, then add the tomatoes. Cook for about 5 minutes, until the tomatoes break up. The sauce should be rather wet, so if the sauce is not juicy, add a little water. Add salt to taste.

Add the monkfish to the sauce, cover, and cook for about 5 minutes, until it begins to lose its translucency. Add the clams, cover, and cook for about 5 minutes. Then add the scallops, cover, and cook for a few minutes more, until they begin to lose their translucency. Add the shrimp, cover, and cook until the shrimp begin to turn pink and the clams begin to open, about 5 minutes.

Remove the lid and add the Foriana sauce. Stir well and cook until the clams are open. (The clams do not have to open their shells wide to be done. Use a knife to coax them open.)

Ladle each serving over a large piece of toasted Italian bread. Serve immediately.

BUTTERFLIED QUAIL WITH FORIANA SAUCE

You can buy D'Artagnan butterflied quail at some gourmet markets and butcher shops or via mail order. If only whole quail is available, butterfly the quail yourself by cutting along the breast with poultry shears. Remove the wishbone by cutting it away from the flesh with a paring knife and spread open the carcass. Quail dries out easily, so be careful not to overcook it.

8 butterflied quail

5 tablespoons olive oil

2 garlic cloves, minced (about 1 tablespoon)

1 tablespoon fresh rosemary leaves

Salt and freshly ground black pepper

¼ pound pancetta or slab bacon, cut into tiny cubes

¾ cup dry white wine

1 teaspoon fresh thyme leaves or a big pinch of dried

1 cup homemade or all-natural low-sodium chicken stock

¼ cup Foriana Sauce

2 tablespoons minced fresh flat-leaf parsley for garnish

SERVES 4

In a large bowl, combine the quail with 3 tablespoons of the olive oil, the garlic, rosemary, and salt and pepper to taste. Mix well. Marinate the quail in the refrigerator for about 30 minutes. Remove the quail from the refrigerator and let it stand in the marinade at room temperature for about 10 minutes.

In the meantime, heat the remaining 2 tablespoons of olive oil in a large skillet over medium heat. Add the pancetta and cook until the fat is rendered, about 10 minutes, stirring often to be sure the pancetta does not burn. Remove the pancetta with a spatula and drain on a paper towel.

Add the quail to the skillet. Be careful: it will spatter. Brown the quail for about 6 minutes on each side. Transfer the quail to a platter and cover with foil to keep it warm.

Add the wine and thyme to the skillet. Cook over medium heat until the wine evaporates, a few minutes, and then add the stock. Scrape the bottom and sides of the skillet to loosen the browned bits as the stock boils gently. (If the stock foams up, turn down the heat a bit.) Cook until the stock is reduced by half, about 10 minutes. Stir in the Foriana sauce. Return the pancetta and quail to the sauce and cook for 5 minutes more, until all the flavors are melded. Sprinkle with parsley to garnish.

Serve immediately, with soft or grilled polenta if you like.

Pork Chops Stuffed with Foriana Sauce

My children love this very tasty dish because of the sweetness of the raisins. To close the stuffing in the chop, use a round toothpick rather than a flat one, as round toothpicks are stronger. Be sure to remove them before serving. I like to serve this dish with baked sweet potatoes.

4 center-cut pork chops, bone-in, about 1½ inches thick

¼ cup Foriana Sauce

¼ cup all-purpose flour

1 tablespoon combined salt and freshly ground black pepper

1 tablespoon unsalted butter

1 cup apple cider, apple juice, warm homemade or all-natural low-sodium chicken stock, dry white wine, or a combination

SERVES 4

Preheat the oven to 350°F.

With the tip of a sharp knife, cut a 2½- to 3-inch-wide slit in the meat to the bone. Insert 1 tablespoon of Foriana sauce into the slit. Close the opening with a toothpick.

In a shallow bowl, stir together the flour and salt and pepper. Mix well. Carefully dredge the chops in the flour.

Heat the butter in a medium cast-iron skillet over medium-high heat. Add 2 chops and brown them for about 5 minutes on each side. Transfer the chops to a roasting pan with a rack and a tight-fitting lid. Brown the remaining chops and transfer them to the rack as well.

Add the cider to the skillet. Scrape the bottom and sides of the skillet to loosen the browned bits as the cider boils gently. Pour the sauce over the chops.

Place the chops in the oven, cover the pan with the lid (or with aluminum foil), and cook for 45 minutes. Allow the chops to rest for a few minutes before serving.

MUSHROOM DUXELLES

Duxelles is a French concoction consisting of minced mushrooms and shallots or onion cooked in butter or oil until the mixture is very soft and dry. It is used for stuffing all kinds of foods: omelets or boned chicken, for example. But it may be most famous as one of the ingredients in beef Wellington. It's a terrific, versatile product, and I like to have it around if only to make a quick savory bruschetta for last-minute company. Mushroom duxelles is packed while still hot in sterilized jars, covered with oil, and refrigerated. Any spoilers that might be in the jar are retarded by refrigeration, and new spoilers can't penetrate the oil layer. (See page 37 for information on preserving in oil.)

MAKES 3 HALF-PINTS

3 tablespoons high-quality Italian olive oil, plus more to cover

6 large shallots, minced (about ¾ cup)

2 pounds white button mushrooms, minced (about 9 cups)

½ cup dry Marsala wine (sweet is good too)

Salt and freshly ground black pepper

Heat 3 tablespoons oil in a large nonstick skillet over medium heat. In batches of about 3 cups, add the shallots and mushrooms and sauté until the mushrooms give up their liquid and the liquid evaporates, about 10 minutes. (Don't cook all the mushrooms and shallots at once, because then the skillet will be crowded and the mushrooms will steam rather than dry out.) Once all the mushrooms and shallots are cooked, return them all to the pan and add the Marsala and salt and pepper to taste. Continue cooking until the duxelles is quite dry and the mushrooms are just beginning to take on a golden color, another 10 minutes.

Bring 3 half-pint jars and their bands to a boil in a large pot of water fitted with a rack. Boil for 10 minutes. Remove the jars with tongs (the tongs don't need to be sterilized). Simmer new lids in a small pan of hot water to soften the rubberized flange. When the jars are dry but still hot, pack the duxelles in as tightly as you can. The more air you push out, the better. Cover with olive oil. Wipe the rims clean of mushroom residue. Set on the lids, screw on the bands, and refrigerate promptly. Check the duxelles a day after you make it: you may need to add more oil to ensure it is completely covered.

The duxelles will be good for about 10 days. To use, pour off the oil, spoon out the amount of duxelles you need, pack the remaining duxelles down into the jar, cover with oil, and return it to the refrigerator.

GREEN OLIVES STUFFED WITH DUXELLES

This dish is a variation of a Marchigiana classic, olives Ascoli-style. The Italians use green olives that have been cured in lime (the mineral, not the fruit), as they are crisper and milder, but you can use any large green olive cured in brine. Just soak them in cold water for several hours before using.

12 large green olives, like Cerignola, soaked in cold water

6 tablespoons Mushroom Duxelles, cold

All-purpose flour for dredging

1 large egg, beaten

Fine fresh bread crumbs for dredging

Vegetable oil (not olive oil) for frying

Salt

Lemon wedges for serving

MAKES 12 STUFFED OLIVES

Pit the olives by paring away the flesh in a long continuous curl from end to end, the way you would peel an orange, or in flaps, and open like the pages of a book. If you cut off a piece by mistake, don't throw it away; you'll still be able to use it.

Form 1 teaspoon of the duxelles into an oblong shape. Carefully wind the olive flesh around the stuffing. You can patch on some of the pieces of olive if you cut off any by mistake. A gentle squeeze will meld the olive and duxelles together. Repeat for the remaining olives.

Have ready 3 plates: one with flour, one with the beaten egg, and one with the bread crumbs. Dredge the stuffed olives in the flour, then dip the olives in the egg until lightly covered, then roll briefly in the bread crumbs. The breaded olives will hold in the refrigerator for a few hours.

When you are ready to serve the olives, heat the oil in a small skillet. Fry the olives until they are golden brown, about 1 minute per side. Drain on paper towels, add salt to taste, and serve with a wedge of lemon.

Chicken Legs Stuffed with Mushroom Duxelles

This dish is very savory and simple to prepare. The only real challenge is boning the leg, which becomes easy after you have done, well, four. In a pinch you can simply cut a pocket next to the thigh bone and stuff the duxelles in there.

4 chicken legs with thighs attached

Generous ¼ cup Mushroom Duxelles

4 large garlic cloves, minced (about 2 tablespoons)

4 sprigs fresh rosemary or 1 tablespoon dried

¼ cup olive oil

Salt and freshly ground black pepper

1 cup dry white wine

SERVES 4

Preheat the oven to 500°F.

Bone each chicken leg, but leave the thigh bone in: Cut the meat around the bottom of the leg bone and push the meat up, like a sock. Separate the leg bone from the thigh bone at the cartilage. Remove the leg bone and pull the meat back down.

Stuff each leg with a heaping tablespoon of duxelles and close the opening with a toothpick or tie it off with a bit of cooking twine. Place the legs in a pan large enough to hold them in a single layer. Sprinkle the legs with the garlic, rosemary, olive oil, and salt and pepper to taste. Roast for 40 minutes. Add the wine and continue cooking for about 15 minutes more, until the chicken is golden brown and the skin looks puffy and crisp.

Remove the toothpick or twine from the chicken legs and serve immediately with the pan drippings poured over the legs.

QUICK BEEF WELLINGTON

This easy, delicious Wellington recipe doesn't call for foie gras, but you can add it if you like: simply place slices of goose liver pâté between the meat and the duxelles. I've tried making this dish with phyllo pastry, but I don't recommend it because the juices from the meat disintegrate the pastry. Puff pastry works best. I use a commercial product, Dufour, which is available at most gourmet shops. You can call 800-439-1282 for retailers that carry it. Traditionally beef Wellington calls for a Bordelaise sauce, but I don't bother with it, as this dish is moist and lovely without it.

1½ pounds beef tenderloin (see Note)

2 tablespoons olive oil

Salt and freshly ground black pepper

14 ounces frozen puff pastry (2 sheets), thawed

4 to 6 tablespoons Mushroom Duxelles

1 large egg, separated

1 tablespoon milk

2 tablespoons chopped fresh flat-leaf parsley for garnish

SERVES 4

Preheat the oven to 425°F.

Brush the tenderloin with the oil. Place the tenderloin in a baking pan in the oven and bake, uncovered, for 25 minutes, until a meat thermometer reads 120°F, for very rare. Remove the meat and add salt and pepper to taste.

Roll out 1 sheet of the puff pastry to a thickness of about ¼ inch on a lightly floured board. Place the pastry on a baking sheet. Place the tenderloin lengthwise in the center of the pastry. Spoon the duxelles over the top of the tenderloin.

Beat the egg white lightly with a fork. Brush the egg white onto the pastry around the perimeter of the meat. Roll out the remaining puff pastry and place it on top of the beef. Press the pastry down to seal. You can crimp the edges of the pastry to make a prettier seal or seal with the flat tines of a fork if you like. Cut the pastry to within an inch of the meat all around. If you like, you can roll out the pastry trimmings and cut out little leaves or designs and, using a bit of egg white, adhere the decorations to the top of the pastry.

Beat the egg yolk and milk together. Brush this mixture over the top of the pastry to create a shiny surface.

Place the Wellington in the oven and cook for 5 minutes, then turn down the heat to 350°F and cook for 10 minutes more, until the pastry is golden brown. Remove the Wellington and let it rest about 10 minutes.

Slice the beef Wellington and garnish with the parsley.

NOTE If you want to beef up the flavor of the Wellington, marinate the beef in a resealable bag with the olive oil, a tablespoon or two of horseradish, a tablespoon of chopped parsley, and salt and pepper for an hour or so.

MUSHROOM DUXELLES >

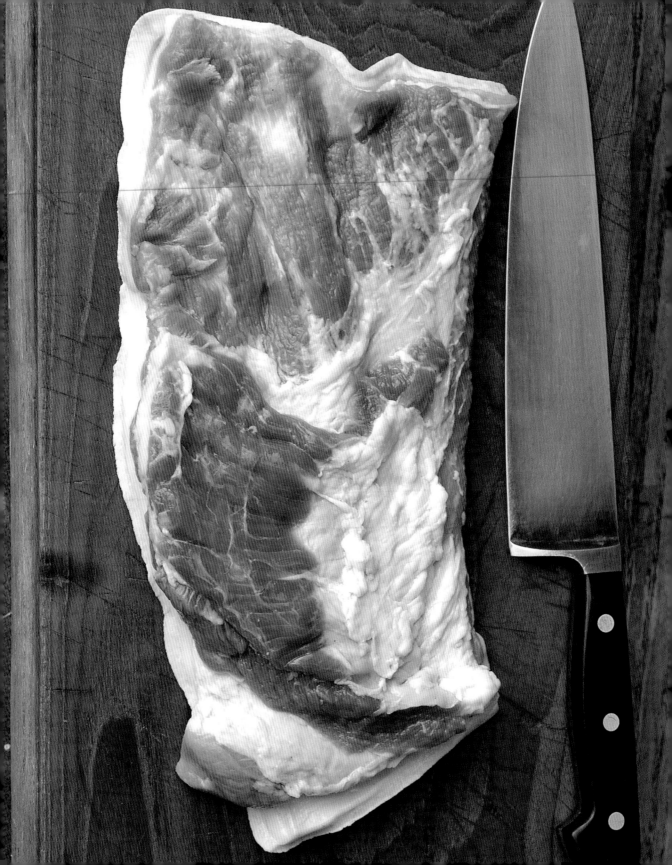

MEAT, POULTRY, AND FISH

BACON

Even though my dad has been curing prosciutto and lonza (the tenderloin of the pig) for many years, it took me a while to feel confident about curing pork. After lots of research I finally figured out a recipe that I was sure was safe, that didn't require nitrite, that I could make in my apartment, and that actually tasted great.

When you smoke bacon, you must use nitrites. In this recipe the bacon is roasted in a low oven after a 1-week curing period, a process that does not require nitrite. The finished bacon must be refrigerated or frozen. It is safe to eat because the curing process kills lots of spoilers, the roasting process kills even more, and refrigeration retards the growth of any spoilers that might remain. The bacon has to be very dry before you wrap and refrigerate it: if you pack it in plastic while it is still warm and moist, mold will grow. (See page 40 for more information on curing meats.)

This is an adaptation of a recipe from *Charcuterie,* by Michael Ruhlman and Brian Polcyn. The spice combination comes, in part, from the Recla speck factory in Alto Adige, Italy. Speck is boned prosciutto that is cured and smoked. The mix of spices is supposedly each producer's secret. However, a young, clearly reckless Recla executive willingly revealed the family formula to me: laurel, juniper, rosemary, caraway, fennel, garlic, and pepper. I substitute thyme for the juniper berries, mainly because I rarely have them on hand. But you should experiment. The addition or subtraction of spices will not affect the safety of the recipe, just the flavor. Don't change the quantity of salt. The sugar merely counterbalances the bitterness of the salt.

MAKES 2½ POUNDS

2½ pounds slab pork belly, skin on (see Note)

3 tablespoons pickling or curing salt

1½ tablespoons sugar

1 tablespoon peppercorns

2 bay leaves

1 large garlic clove, minced

1 teaspoon fennel seed

1 teaspoon caraway seed

1 teaspoon dried rosemary

1 teaspoon dried thyme

Wash and dry the meat. Place it on a large sheet of wax paper.

In a spice grinder, a coffee grinder, or with a mortar and pestle, mix together the salt, sugar, peppercorns, bay leaves, garlic, fennel, caraway, rosemary, and thyme. Grind to the consistency of kosher salt (some of the seasoning ingredients will become powdery—it's okay).

Rub the seasonings all over the meat. Place the meat in a large resealable plastic freezer bag. Dump all of the remaining seasoning into the bag and shake it around to distribute it throughout. Refrigerate the bacon, turning the bag over periodically, for 7 days. Brine will develop in the bag. It won't be sopping wet, but you will see puddles of water in the bag. This is good.

After the 7 days are up, remove the pork belly, wash it, and dry it very well. Place the meat in a baking dish and cover with plastic wrap or foil.

Refrigerate for 24 hours. This allows the salt to distribute evenly throughout the meat.

Preheat the oven to 200°F. Pour any accumulated moisture out of the baking dish (there won't be much, if any). Place the meat, uncovered, back in the baking dish. Roast for 2 to 2½ hours, until the internal temperature of the meat is 150°F. The bacon will smell spicy and strong and be brown all over. If you cook the bacon too long, the meat will become tough and the fat will render, creating as much as ½ cup of rendered fat in the bottom of the pan and causing the rind to stick (obviously I've made this mistake). Best to check the internal temperature of the bacon with a meat thermometer after about 1½ hours.

When the meat is cool enough to handle, cut off the rind. Dry the meat very well and wrap in wax paper before placing in a bag in the refrigerator, where it will keep for about 2 weeks.

Cut the rind into chunks and freeze; they add excellent flavor to soups. I like to cut about half the bacon into 1-cup bags of lardons and freeze them individually; they'll keep for 3 months in the freezer.

NOTE Some butchers will sell you a pork belly that has been folded. This does not affect the flavor, but the crease in the rind can cause the bacon to buckle. To avoid this, weight the bacon down during the 7-day curing process. Place the bagged meat in a baking pan and place a smaller baking pan on top, then load on the weight. I use a brick. Every time you turn over the meat, replace the weight.

FRISÉE SALAD WITH POACHED EGGS AND LARDONS

There is nothing particularly exotic about this bistro standby—until you taste it with your own homemade lardons. It becomes a totally different dish at that point: savory, salty, and flavored with a bit of hot, delicious fat. You can substitute baby arugula or watercress for the frisée if you like. This dish is excellent with a fine white wine. Lately I've been drinking Qupé wines from Santa Maria, California. The whole line is yummy.

FOR THE VINAIGRETTE

1 tablespoon minced shallot

1 teaspoon mustard

1 tablespoon fresh lemon juice or white wine vinegar

Salt and freshly ground black pepper

4 to 6 tablespoons vegetable oil (not olive oil)

FOR THE SALAD

¾ pound Bacon, cut into lardons (narrow pieces about ½ inch long), about 2 cups

1 teaspoon distilled white vinegar

8 large fresh organic eggs

1 pound frisée, washed and dried

Salt and freshly ground black pepper

SERVES 4

Prepare the vinaigrette. Combine the shallot, mustard, lemon juice, and salt and pepper to taste in a medium bowl. Whisk as you slowly dribble in the oil. When it is thickened and has a mild yet snappy taste, set it aside.

Sauté the bacon in a skillet over medium heat until the lardons are browned and the fat is rendered, about 10 minutes. Keep warm.

Bring a medium pot of water to a boil and then turn it down to a simmer. Add the white vinegar. Swirl the water to create a maelstrom. Crack the eggs, one at a time, into a ramekin and then slide the eggs into the center of the twirling water. Cook for about 2 minutes, until the whites are opaque. Remove carefully with a slotted spoon. I usually try to prepare 2 eggs at a time so there is less opportunity for the eggs to get cold. If you have an egg poacher, even better.

Toss the frisée in the vinaigrette and distribute it among 4 shallow bowls. Place 2 eggs on top of each salad and then spoon over equal portions of lardons and hot oil. Sprinkle the eggs with a bit of salt and the entire salad with freshly ground black pepper.

RIGATONI WITH BACON, DATES, AND GORGONZOLA

When my husband first tasted this dish he said it was weird but lovely. It *is* unusual. But the warm, rich flavors pull together very nicely—it has a holidaylike quality. I like to serve it with a peppery green salad made with watercress and arugula. This is a great wine dish. We eat it with Italian wines from Tuscany like Chianti Classico, Vino Nobile di Montepulciano, and, when we are feeling flush, Brunello. Made primarily from the Sangiovese grape, they are medium-bodied, earthy wines.

1 teaspoon olive oil

¾ pound Bacon, cut into lardons (narrow pieces about ½ inch long), about 2 cups

¾ pound rigatoni or, if you can find it, mezzi-rigatoni (they're smaller)

½ cup chopped pitted dates

¼ cup grated Parmesan cheese

½ cup crumbled Gorgonzola cheese

3 tablespoons minced fresh flat-leaf parsley for garnish

SERVES 4

Heat the oil in a medium skillet over medium heat. Add the bacon and cook until the fat is rendered and the bacon is browned, 10 to 15 minutes. Set aside but do not drain.

Bring a large pot of salted water to a boil over high heat. Add the pasta and cook until it is al dente. Drain but reserve about ¾ cup of the pasta water. Dump the pasta into a serving bowl and moisten with the hot pasta water, about ¼ cup at a time. The pasta should be moist, not wet.

In the meantime, reheat the bacon over medium-low heat and add the dates to warm through, about 5 minutes. Add the bacon and dates to the pasta and toss to combine. Add the Parmesan cheese and a little more of the pasta water if the dish seems too dry. Add the Gorgonzola cheese and toss. Garnish with the parsley and serve.

CHICKEN CANZANESE

This dish, originally from Abruzzi, is an adaptation of my dad's recipe. I love it because you simply assemble the ingredients in the pan, cover, and cook. There's no fussing with it after assembly. It is important, though, that you brine the chicken first so the meat does not dry out. Lately I've been using skinned and boned thighs, in which case, you don't have to brine them. Plus they cook a bit more quickly.

8 chicken thighs or one 3-pound chicken cut into serving pieces

1 tablespoon salt

½ pound Bacon, cut into lardons (narrow pieces about ½ inch long), about 1½ cups

½ cup dry white wine

4 garlic cloves, thinly sliced (about 2 tablespoons)

4 fresh sage leaves, minced

3 fresh sprigs rosemary (about 3 inches long)

2 bay leaves

12 peppercorns, crushed

1 hot dried chile, about 2 inches long

SERVES 4

Brine the chicken: Place the chicken parts in a bowl with 2 quarts of water and the salt. Refrigerate for 1 hour. Drain the chicken, return it to the bowl, and cover with fresh water. Allow the chicken to rest in the fresh water for about 10 minutes. Drain and pat dry with paper towels.

Place the chicken in a large braising pan with a tight-fitting cover. Add the bacon, wine, ¼ cup water, garlic, sage, rosemary, bay leaves, peppercorns, and chile to the pan with the chicken. Cover and bring to a boil, then reduce the heat and simmer over medium heat for 40 minutes, checking periodically to make sure the sauce doesn't completely evaporate. If it is about to, then add equal parts wine and water to moisten.

Remove the cover and turn the heat up to high. Cook for a few minutes to brown the chicken and reduce the liquid. Serve immediately.

SMOKED CHICKEN BREASTS

These breasts are tasty and versatile: wonderful in a sandwich, thrown into a cassoulet, or in a multitude of salad dishes.

Chicken breasts are preserved by curing with salt, which inhibits the growth of bacteria, and by the application of heat from the smoke, which kills bacteria, after which they must be refrigerated to ensure what bacteria is left doesn't grow. I use a Camerons stovetop smoker and find it works equally well on gas and ceramic stovetops. A variety of wood chips should come with your smoker, and you can buy additional chips through the manufacturer. (See page 40 for information on curing and smoking.)

Smoked chicken breasts will hold for about 2 weeks in the refrigerator.

MAKES 3 WHOLE BREASTS

1 cup pickling salt

½ cup brown sugar, packed

3 whole boneless, skinless chicken breasts, halved (about 3 pounds)

1½ tablespoons hickory chips

4 tablespoons (½ stick) cold unsalted butter

Place 3 quarts of water in a nonreactive bowl and whisk in the salt and sugar until dissolved. Place the breasts in the water. Be sure they are totally submerged. If they are not, fill a freezer bag with 6 cups of water and ½ cup pickling salt and place it on top. (The brine bag will serve as a weight to keep the breasts submerged, and if the bag leaks, it will release only brine.) Cover the bowl with plastic wrap and refrigerate for 24 hours. This step is brining, and it is important because to store smoked chicken in the refrigerator safely, you need to introduce salt into the flesh. Salt is the primary preservative of smoked chicken.

Remove the breasts, rinse them with cold water, and return them to a bowl filled with cold water. Allow the breasts to soak for 2 hours in the refrigerator. This is called *clearing,* and it helps the salt distribute equally throughout the flesh (so it's not too salty on the outside). Drain, rinse, and pat the breasts dry. Smoke does not deposit well on wet flesh.

Check the lid on your smoker to ensure it fits snugly. Place the chips under the smoking pan and the rack over the smoking pan. Place the breasts on

FARFALLE WITH SMOKED CHICKEN AND BABY ARUGULA >

the rack. Cut up the butter and distribute it evenly over the top of the breasts (see Note). Place the smoker over medium heat and slide the top in place, leaving it open a small crack. When you see wisps of smoke escaping from the crack, close the lid firmly and turn the heat down to medium-low. If smoke still leaks out around the edges of the lid, wrap the lid with a damp dish towel. Sometimes I put a kettle of water on top if the lid is warping (this happens a lot with my stovetop smoker). It is important that the smoke stay in the smoker; otherwise the chicken will not get hot enough to cook. Smoke the breasts for 20 minutes per pound, about 1 hour. You will hear the butter sizzle and smell the chicken cooking.

Turn off the heat and allow the smoker to come down to room temperature. Remove the breasts and wrap them in paper towels and then in wax paper. Don't wrap the warm breasts in plastic to refrigerate: the moisture on the breasts will condense and speed up the growth of mold. Store in the refrigerator for up to about 2 weeks.

NOTE At this stage you can experiment with other flavors. For example, instead of butter, sprinkle paprika or chili powder over the breasts.

LENTIL SOUP WITH SMOKED CHICKEN

This recipe is adapted from one my dad published in his first book, *Italian Family Cooking* (Random House, 1971; that's me on the back cover in the braids). The smoked chicken lends a nice earthy note to the soup, and the little hunk of Parmesan lends richness.

½ cup dried brown lentils

½ carrot, chopped

1 celery stalk, chopped

1 whole garlic clove, peeled

1 small onion, chopped

3 tablespoons chopped tomato

One 2-inch-square hunk Parmesan cheese

Pinch of dried oregano

½ Smoked Chicken Breast, sliced (3 to 4 ounces)

1 small potato, peeled and diced

Salt and freshly ground black pepper

1 teaspoon chopped fresh flat-leaf parsley

SERVES 4

Put the lentils, carrot, celery, garlic, onion, tomato, Parmesan, oregano, and 3 cups water into a soup pot and bring to a boil. Reduce the heat to medium-low and cook gently for 1¼ hours. Add the chicken and potato and, when the potato is tender, remove the garlic. Season with salt and pepper. Serve hot, sprinkled with parsley.

Farfalle with Smoked Chicken and Baby Arugula

This is a fresh-tasting, simple pasta dish, excellent for company, as the ingredients are best tossed together at the last minute. (If you combine the ingredients ahead of time, the vinaigrette will make the arugula soggy.) You can also prepare this dish as a salad, omitting the pasta. You can also use watercress instead of baby arugula—the result is delightful.

¾ pound farfalle or other flat, cut pasta like taccole (my favorite but hard to find)

1 large shallot, minced (about 2 tablespoons)

1 tablespoon fresh lemon juice

1 teaspoon Dijon mustard

¼ cup vegetable oil (not olive oil)

Salt and freshly ground black pepper

2 Smoked Chicken Breast halves, chopped into bite-sized pieces (about 3 cups)

½ pound baby arugula, washed

¼ cup grated Parmesan cheese

Extra virgin olive oil for garnish, optional

SERVES 4

Bring a large pot of salted water to a boil over high heat. Add the pasta and cook until al dente. Drain.

In the meantime, make the vinaigrette. In a small bowl, whisk together the shallot, lemon juice, and mustard. Slowly add the oil, whisking all the time. The vinaigrette will become creamy as the oil emulsifies. Add salt and pepper to taste.

Pour the hot drained pasta into a serving bowl. Add the vinaigrette 1 tablespoon at a time, until the pasta is well dressed. Toss in the smoked chicken and arugula. Add the Parmesan cheese and a dribble of extra virgin olive oil, if you like, and a few more grinds of black pepper. Serve immediately.

SMOKED CHICKEN AND WILD RICE SALAD

This is a sweet salad that I love to serve warm, although it is excellent served at room temperature and holds in the refrigerator quite well.

1 cup wild rice

1 teaspoon salt

¼ cup slivered blanched almonds

2 Smoked Chicken Breast halves, cut into bite-sized pieces (about 3 cups)

2 tablespoons golden raisins

1 tablespoon fresh lemon juice

2 to 3 tablespoons olive oil

Freshly ground black pepper

2 tablespoons minced fresh flat-leaf parsley for garnish

SERVES 4

Preheat the oven to 400°F.

Place the rice in a medium saucepan and add 1 quart of water and the salt. Bring to a boil over medium-high heat. Cover and turn the heat down to a simmer. Cook for 40 minutes, until the rice is tender. Toss with the tines of a fork and pour into a serving bowl.

In the meantime, place the almonds on a cookie sheet and place in the hot oven. Toast until they are golden and fragrant, about 2 minutes. Remove and add to the serving bowl with the wild rice.

Add the chicken, raisins, lemon juice, oil, and pepper to the bowl and toss. You probably will not need any salt, but check the seasoning and adjust to your taste. Garnish with the minced parsley.

CANNED TUNA

I always can tuna in the fall, when the western Atlantic fish are at their optimum weight, having migrated north all summer long, feasting on smaller fish. I often make twelve jars at a time because I know how good this tuna is. If you want to do the same, just double the recipe—the times and pressure stay the same. I use the tuna in composed salads; to make a tangy, creamy sauce for veal; in a variety of pasta dishes, either as the primary flavor or as an addition to a very tasty room-temperature pasta with pesto, boiled green beans, potatoes, and scallions; and in sandwiches. Home-canned tuna is much more delicate than commercial and has no fishy taste.

You can preserve any cut of tuna and any grade, although the fattier the tuna, the more tender and flavorful. Tuna needs to age for 3 to 6 months to mellow the flavor, after which it is good for a year. Canned tuna is a low-acid food, so it must be pressure canned. Pressure canning brings the interior temperature up high enough to kill all spoilers that might be present in the flesh. Because of the expense of tuna, it can be very disappointing if the seals fail. This happened to me only once (we ended up eating a lot of delicious refrigerated tuna over the next few weeks as a result), and I figured out it was because I had not left enough headspace in the jar. You must leave $3/4$ inch of headspace above the oil for a proper seal. (See page 28 for information on pressure canning.)

MAKES 6 HALF-PINTS

3½ pounds very fresh tuna, with skin, bones, and any stringy blood vessels removed

1 tablespoon kosher salt

Italian olive oil (not extra virgin)

Have ready 6 scalded half-pint jars and their bands. (To scald, simply dip the jars in boiling water. You don't need to sterilize the jars, as you will be processing them for over 10 minutes.) Simmer new lids in a small pan of hot water to soften the rubberized flange.

Cut the tuna into chunks as close in size to your jars as you can manage. Stuff the chunks of tuna into the jar and fill the gaps in the jars with small bits of tuna, still leaving 1 inch of headspace at the top. Do not overfill the jars or your seals will fail.

Add ½ teaspoon of salt to the top of each jar and pour in enough olive oil to cover the fish, leaving ¾ inch of headspace at the top of the jar. Using a butter knife, press the tuna away from the sides of the jar so the oil can fill any air pockets between the chunks of tuna.

Wipe the rims, set on the lids, and screw on the bands fingertip tight. (If you put a dab of white vinegar on the cloth you use to wipe the rims, the oil will clean off better.)

Place the rack in the bottom of your pressure canner. Place 2 to 3 inches of boiling water in the bottom of your pressure canner. Add 1 teaspoon of white vinegar if you like: it will keep your jars sparkling clean. Place the jars on the rack. Align the cover handles so they are locked into position as per the instructions for your pressure canner. Remove the pressure regulator from the steam vent. Heat the canner over high heat. Allow steam to be released from the vent for 7 to 10 minutes and then put the pressure regulator over the steam vent. Watch the pressure regulator. When it is about to reach 10 pounds of pressure, lower the heat slightly so that once it reaches 10 pounds it stays there. Check periodically to ensure the pressure stays at 10 pounds. Usually, once you've got the heat right, the pressure will become stable. If you are a little over, it's okay.

Just don't go under 10 pounds. (If the pressure dips under 10 pounds, you can't count those minutes against the time you must process the fish. Stop timing, bring the canner back up to pressure by increasing the heat, and then continue timing.) Process the jars at 10 pounds of pressure for 100 minutes.

Turn off the heat and allow the pressure to drop naturally. When the canner is depressurized (the pressure regulator will read 0), remove the gauge, then the top. Open the top of the pressure canner away from you, as there still may be some hot air inside. Remove the jars and allow them to rest for at least 6 hours. If you didn't use vinegar inside the pressure canner, the jars may be greasy. It's okay—just wipe them down with a rag doused in white vinegar. Check the seals and store in a cool, dark place. Tuna needs to age for 3 to 6 months to mellow the flavor. Refrigerate after opening.

NOTE If little crystals form on the inside of your jars, don't worry; it's safe to eat. This is magnesium ammonium phosphate, a naturally occurring mineral in fish that crystallizes under certain conditions. It usually dissolves when heated. You may also see little bits of creamy white matter in the jars. Lucky you! This is fat, and fat is good.

WARM POTATO AND TUNA SALAD

The basic recipe for this fine luncheon or dinner salad is tuna, boiled potatoes, lemon juice, olive oil, and parsley. But at different times I've added fresh tarragon, basil, mint, cilantro, or onion grass; marinated mushrooms, marinated artichokes, sliced red onion, chopped olives, chopped scallions, boiled green beans, chopped fresh tomatoes. . . . Lots of ingredients will work in various combinations, making this as versatile as it is tasty. I love this dish with white Loire Valley wines.

2 pounds small potatoes (I like Yukon Gold and German Butterball)

2 half-pints canned Tuna

Juice of 1 lemon (about 2 tablespoons)

Extra virgin olive oil

Salt and freshly ground black pepper

2 tablespoons minced fresh flat-leaf parsley

SERVES 4

Bring a large pot of salted water to a boil over high heat. Throw in the potatoes and cook until tender, 10 to 15 minutes. Drain the potatoes and, when they are cool enough to handle, peel off the skins and slice.

Place the potatoes in a serving bowl and add the tuna with its oil, the lemon juice, and, if the oil from the tuna is not enough to make the potatoes shine, a little extra virgin olive oil. Add salt and pepper to taste. Garnish with the parsley. Serve warm or at room temperature.

Spaghettini with Tuna

I make this dish often, as it is super-fast and easy but tastes fancy. Bottarga, the smoked roe of the red mullet, is an expensive product. It is sold in a jar as a powder or whole and vacuum packed, and it is very sexy and worth a try. Bottarga is traditionally added to a simple spaghetti al'olio (olive oil, garlic, salt, and pepper), which is basically what this dish is, with the addition of tuna fish. My dad makes this dish with black cuttlefish ink pasta and anchovies—it's terrific.

3 tablespoons olive oil

6 large garlic cloves, minced (about 3 tablespoons)

Hot red pepper flakes

2 half-pints Canned Tuna

¾ pound spaghettini

1 cup homemade or all-natural low-sodium chicken stock, or a little more if needed

Salt

¼ cup grated bottarga

Extra virgin olive oil for garnish, optional

2 tablespoons minced fresh flat-leaf parsley

SERVES 4

Heat the oil in a large skillet over medium-low heat. Add the garlic and hot red pepper flakes to taste and cook until the garlic is fragrant, 2 to 3 minutes. Add the tuna with its oil and continue cooking, breaking up the tuna with a spoon, for about 2 minutes. Set aside.

Bring a large pot of salted water to a boil over high heat. Add the spaghettini and cook until al dente; then drain. Add the spaghettini to the pan with the tuna.

Toss the spaghettini in the tuna sauce over medium-low heat. Add the chicken stock and continue tossing for about 2 minutes. (You may need a bit more stock—add enough to make the pasta slick.) Add salt to taste.

Garnish the pasta with the bottarga and, if you like, a dribble of extra virgin olive oil, along with the minced parsley.

NOTE You can also add a couple of tablespoons of Green Olive Tapenade (page 71) if you have it on hand.

VITELLO TONNATO

This is a quickie version of the Italian classic, and it tastes no less wonderful for being so easy. The tuna sauce is also good on pasta, garnished with lots of chopped parsley. This makes an excellent summer supper.

2 pounds boneless veal loin

Salt and freshly ground black pepper

3 tablespoons olive oil

½ cup plus ⅓ cup homemade or all-natural low-sodium chicken stock

1 half-pint Canned Tuna, drained

1 tablespoon fresh lemon juice

1 small garlic clove, minced

½ pound baby arugula, washed, optional

Extra virgin olive oil, optional

½ lemon, thinly sliced crosswise

1 tablespoon drained capers

SERVES 4

Preheat the oven to 350°F.

Season the loin all over with salt and pepper to taste. Heat 2 tablespoons of the oil in a large skillet over high heat. Add the veal loin and brown it all over, about 10 minutes. Transfer the loin to a baking pan with a rack. Add ½ cup of the stock to the skillet you browned the meat in and scrape with a wooden spoon to release the browned bits. Pour the stock over the veal. Roast the veal in the middle of the oven for 35 minutes for medium-rare. Let it rest at room temperature for at least 10 minutes, then chill in the refrigerator.

In the meantime, place the tuna, lemon juice, garlic, remaining tablespoon of olive oil, and salt and pepper to taste in a food processor. Puree, slowly pouring in the remaining ⅓ cup stock. Pour the sauce into a bowl and chill in the refrigerator.

When you are ready to serve, slice the veal as thinly as you can. (I use a very long, narrow blade with a rounded end.) I serve the slices on a platter atop baby arugula that has been dressed with salt and a dribble of olive oil, but traditionally, the veal is served on its own. Either way, pour the sauce over the veal and garnish with lemon slices and capers.

GRAVLAX

I have tried various gravlax recipes over the years, and this one is the best. It draws from two sources, a recipe given to me by the former *Gourmet* restaurant critic Jay Jacobs and one given to me by my friend Warren Ser in Miami (who got it from a Swedish pal). Choose salmon fillets from the center of the fish: they're meatier. Gravlax is great to have around as an hors d'oeuvre, served with rye crisps, emulsified mustard, and lemon wedges, but I quickly tire of eating it this way. So when I make this dish for a party, the next couple of days are filled with easy, fast, gravlax-spiked dishes. Gravlax is cured in salt (salt wreaks havoc on spoilers) and is refrigerated (which retards spoilers). It lasts in the refrigerator for 10 days. (See page 40 for information on curing.)

MAKES TWO 1-POUND FILLETS

2½ pounds salmon, cut into 2 fillets with the skin on, preferably from the same fish so the fillets fit together neatly

⅔ cup sugar

⅓ cup kosher salt

1 tablespoon coarsely ground white pepper (commercial powdered is okay)

1 bunch fresh dill

2 tablespoons dill seeds

If you're using wild salmon, place the fillets in the freezer for 7 days at -10°F or 15 hours at -31°F before preparing gravlax or buy frozen wild salmon. Freezing kills any parasites that may be present in the fish. Farm-raised salmon is unlikely to carry parasites. (I prefer organic Scottish farm-raised. It's fatty and makes a luscious gravlax.)

Be sure the salmon you buy stays chilled up until the moment you cure it: about 38°F is ideal. Wash the fillets. Lay the fillets down and feel them gently with your fingers to find the bones. Remove any bones with needle-nosed pliers or tweezers. Be careful to avoid bruising the salmon.

Combine the sugar, salt, and pepper in a bowl.

Lay a large sheet of plastic wrap on the counter. Lay one salmon fillet on top of it, skin side down. Sprinkle half the sugar-spice mixture onto the fish. Repeat with the other fillet. Gently rub as much of the salt mixture into the flesh as you can without bruising the meat (you won't be able to rub it all in). Cover one fillet with half of the fresh dill so that it is completely covered. (It's okay to leave the stems on.) Sprinkle the dill seeds over the fresh dill and then add the remaining fresh dill. Place the other fillet directly on top. Some of the salt and sugar mixture will fall off. Pack any extra salt/sugar, as well as salt/

GRAVLAX AND SHAVED FENNEL SALAD

sugar that you weren't able to rub into the flesh, around the fish. Securely wrap the plastic wrap around the fish and then wrap more plastic around the fish so that it is snug. Place the fish in a resealable plastic bag, press out the air, and fold the bag tightly around the fish. The salt pulls the water out of the tissue of the fish and dissolves in these juices to create a brine. It is important that the juices produced by salting the fish do not escape, as gravlax must baste in its brine to cure.

Place the fish in a pan and put weights on top of it, like a few bricks in resealable plastic bags or canned goods. You can also load a heavy bag of rice or beans on top. To distribute the weight evenly, place a pan on top of the fish and fill it with the weight.

Place the fish in the refrigerator. It needs to cure for at least 48 and up to 60 hours. (You will get a more tender gravlax by curing for 48 to 52 hours.) Turn the fish over every 12 hours. You can write "day" with a felt-tip pen on one side and "night" on the other, as it is easy to forget how often you have turned the fish.

After at least 48 hours, remove the plastic wrap from around the fish. The fillets will have reduced in thickness by almost half. Scrape off the dill and dill seeds and wipe the fish clean. If there is a white film on the fish, don't worry: it is impurities that have been drawn from the flesh by the salt. Just wipe it off with a clean cloth. The fish can be eaten at this point. However, you can add the following flavorings, which are very good.

Rub 1 tablespoon of aquavit into each fillet, then pat a freshly ground mix of ½ teaspoon white pepper, 1 teaspoon black pepper, 2 teaspoons coriander seeds, 2 teaspoons fennel seeds, and 2 teaspoons caraway seeds into the fish. You can also coat the fish with finely chopped dill.

Wrap the fish in wax paper; it will keep in the fridge for 10 days.

To slice gravlax, lay the fillet on a cutting board, skin side down. With a long, flexible knife, slice paper-thin pieces on a diagonal. Start slicing the fish at the top of the fillet, about a third of the way down the length of the fish, sliding the blade toward the skin as you go. If you cut pieces straight up and down, you will find yourself sawing through the tough skin. You can preslice the fish and keep it in the refrigerator in wax paper, but the slices will dry out much faster than if you slice to order.

Gravlax and Shaved Fennel Salad

This is a very pretty, tasty dish I make during the winter when the fennel is in. You can also make this dish in the summer with shaved seeded cucumber. I use a mandoline to shave the fennel into almost translucent strips.

2 fennel bulbs (about 1 pound), greens and core removed, shaved

12 slices Gravlax (about ½ pound), cut into 2-inch pieces

1 teaspoon Dijon mustard

1 tablespoon fresh lemon juice

Salt and freshly ground black pepper

¼ cup light oil, like safflower

2 tablespoons minced fresh chives or dill

SERVES 4 AS AN APPETIZER

In a small bowl, combine the shaved fennel and the gravlax.

Prepare the vinaigrette: Whisk the mustard, lemon juice, and salt and pepper to taste together. Add the oil in a slow dribble, whisking all the while, until you have used all the oil and the vinaigrette thickens.

Toss the fennel and gravlax in the vinaigrette. Gently pile a quarter of the salad onto each of 4 small plates. Garnish each salad with chives.

Farfalle Alfredo with Gravlax

Sweet, rich, and delectable, this dish is terrific followed by a green salad, which cleanses the palate of residual cream. Farfalle, which means "butterfly" in Italian, is bow tie pasta. The flat surface of the pasta is particularly suitable for creamy sauces, which needs some real estate to cling to.

6 tablespoons (¾ stick) unsalted butter

1 large onion, minced (about 1½ cups)

2 cups heavy cream

Heaping ¼ teaspoon freshly grated nutmeg

Salt and freshly ground black or white pepper

12 slices Gravlax, cut into 2-inch pieces, plus ¼ cup minced Gravlax

¾ pound farfalle or other wide flat pasta like pappardelle

⅓ cup grated Parmesan cheese

2 tablespoons minced fresh dill

SERVES 4

Melt the butter in a small saucepan over medium-low heat. Add the onion and cook for 5 minutes, until translucent. Do not brown. Add the cream and simmer until the cream is reduced by half, 20 to 25 minutes. Do not let the cream come to a high boil, just a low bubble, and stir down the foam every couple of minutes. Once the cream starts to thicken, add the nutmeg and salt and pepper to taste. Add the slices of gravlax and cook for about 2 minutes more, until the gravlax is warmed through. The gravlax will turn a powder pink as it cooks.

In the meantime, bring a large pot of salted water to a boil over high heat. Add the farfalle and cook until it is al dente. Drain the pasta and pour it onto a serving platter. Add the cream sauce and Parmesan cheese and toss well. Garnish with the dill and ¼ cup of minced gravlax. Serve immediately.

EGGS WITH GRAVLAX

This dish is lovely served in a nest of puff pastry. (I use frozen Dufour puff pastry; call 800-439-1282 to find retailers.) To make a pastry nest, defrost 2 sheets of puff pastry. Fold each sheet over in half and cut into circles about 5 inches in diameter. Score a smaller, 3-inch-diameter circle in the center of each circle and bake according to the instructions on the box. When the pastry is puffed up and golden, remove the center and deposit the eggs with gravlax inside. Otherwise, the eggs are very good served with hot buttered croissants and a Bloody Mary made with aquavit.

4 tablespoons (½ stick) unsalted butter

4 garlic cloves, minced, or 3 shallots, minced

12 large eggs, beaten

¼ cup sour cream

Salt and freshly ground black pepper

12 slices Gravlax, cut into 2-inch-long pieces

3 tablespoons minced fresh dill

SERVES 4

Melt the butter in a medium nonstick pan over medium-low heat. Add the garlic and cook until fragrant, about 1 minute. Add the eggs. Allow them to set for a few seconds and then stir slowly until the eggs are almost done to your taste. Add the sour cream, salt and pepper to taste, and the gravlax. Cook, folding gently, for a few seconds more. The salmon will lighten in color to a powder pink as it cooks.

Serve the eggs garnished with the dill and a few grinds of black pepper.

SMOKED SCALLOPS

The versatility of smoked scallops cannot be underestimated. For a quick appetizer, I serve a few on top of a puddle of green sauce made by blending together a handful of leafy herbs, a tablespoon of pine nuts, and a few garlic cloves in a food processor. Smoked scallops are fabulous dropped into a bean soup, excellent tossed with marinated mushrooms, and great in a potato salad with scallions and garlic mayonnaise. The scallops will hold for 10 days in the fridge—but you'll be lucky to have them around that long once you taste them.

Smoked scallops are preserved by curing with salt, which inhibits the growth of bacteria, and by the application of heat from the smoke, which kills bacteria, after which they must be refrigerated to ensure what bacteria are left don't grow. I use a Camerons stovetop smoker and find it works equally well on gas and ceramic stovetops. A variety of wood chips should come with your smoker, and you can buy additional chips through the manufacturer. (See page 40 for information on curing and smoking.)

MAKES ABOUT 1½ POUNDS

1 cup pickling salt

3 pounds medium dry-pack scallops
(about 20 per pound), abductor muscle removed
(see Note)

1½ tablespoons alder chips (or other wood
chips of your choosing, as long as they are
processed by the manufacturer of
your smoker)

Combine the salt and 7 cups cold water and mix to dissolve the salt. (You can use kosher salt, too, but you will find it doesn't dissolve as well.) Drop in the scallops and let them rest in the refrigerator for an hour. This step is called *brining,* and it is important because to store smoked fish in the refrigerator safely, you need to introduce salt into the flesh. Salt is the primary preservative of smoked fish.

Drain and rinse the scallops and return them to the bowl with clean cold water. Allow the scallops to soak for about 30 minutes. This is called *clearing,* and it helps the salt to distribute evenly throughout the scallop (so it's not too salty on the outside). Drain, rinse, and pat dry the scallops. Smoke does not deposit well on wet flesh.

Place the wood chips in the bottom of the smoker and the tray and grill on top. Place the scallops on the grill. Leave the smoker open a crack and place it over medium heat. As soon as you see wisps of smoke escaping, close the smoker. Smoke the scallops for 35 minutes. Some smoke will find a way

< EGGS WITH SMOKED SCALLOPS

out of the smoker during the first 5 minutes or so. It's okay. It will usually stop. If it doesn't, wrap the lid with a damp dish towel. Sometimes I put a kettle of water on top if the lid is warping (this happens a lot with my stovetop smoker). It is important that the smoke stay in the smoker; otherwise the scallops will not get hot enough to cook.

After 35 minutes, turn off the heat and allow the smoker to come to room temperature. Remove the scallops. (I highly recommend you eat a few while they are still warm. They're luscious.) Let the scallops come down to room temperature, then dry them off and place in a plastic container lined with a paper towel. Don't place warm scallops in a plastic bag or container: the moisture on the scallops will condense and speed up the growth of mold.

NOTE The scallop has a small tough muscle attached to its body called the *abductor*. It is easy to spot because it is usually a little darker than the rest of the scallop. It pulls off easily. Dry-pack scallops are scallops that have not been treated with chemicals to make them retain water.

SMOKED SCALLOPS ALLA CARBONARA

My husband, Kevin, came up with this easy-to-prepare recipe, and it is a winner. We often serve the kids this dish without the scallops, then add the scallops for the adults.

3 tablespoons olive oil or unsalted butter

2 medium onions, chopped (about 2 cups)

2 large garlic cloves, chopped (about 1 tablespoon)

¾ pound spaghetti

2 large eggs

Salt and freshly ground black pepper

1 cup grated Parmesan cheese

½ pound Smoked Scallops (about 20), cut into bite-sized pieces

3 tablespoons chopped fresh flat-leaf parsley

SERVES 4

Heat the oil in a large skillet over medium heat. Add the onions and garlic and cook until the onions become translucent, about 5 minutes.

Bring a large pot of salted water to a boil over high heat. Add the spaghetti and cook until al dente.

In the meantime, break the eggs in the bottom of a serving bowl and whisk until slightly frothy. Add salt and black pepper to taste.

When the pasta is al dente, drain it and dump it into the bowl with the eggs. Using tongs, mix well. It is important that you add the pasta to the eggs immediately after draining, as the heat from the pasta cooks the eggs. Add the sautéed onions and the cheese and combine. Add the scallops and toss gently. Garnish with parsley and serve immediately.

EGGS WITH SMOKED SCALLOPS

Pile these eggs on toasted Italian bread that's been rubbed with oil and sprinkled with salt.

6 tablespoons (¾ stick) unsalted butter

4 large garlic cloves, minced (about 2 tablespoons), or ¼ cup minced shallot

12 large organic eggs

Salt and freshly ground black pepper

½ pound Smoked Scallops (about 20)

¼ cup minced fresh tarragon

SERVES 4

Heat 4 tablespoons of the butter in a large nonstick skillet over medium-low heat. Do not brown. Add the garlic and cook until fragrant, about 1 minute. Do not brown the garlic. Crack in the eggs. Add salt and black pepper to taste. Allow them to cook until the whites become opaque, about 45 seconds, then scramble them. When they are still very soft, add the scallops and half the tarragon. Fold in the scallops and finish cooking the eggs. I like them soft, about 2 minutes.

To serve family style, dump the eggs onto a platter and garnish with the remaining tarragon and bits of the remaining 2 tablespoons of butter, with toast on the side. To serve individually, place a piece of toast on the plate, put the eggs on top, and then garnish with tarragon and ½ tablespoon of butter per serving. You can also dribble with extra virgin olive oil or white truffle oil.

SCALLOPS DAUPHINOIS

This is dynamite served next to a grilled steak.

2 cups heavy cream

4 baking potatoes, peeled and cut into ⅛-inch-thick slices

3 garlic cloves, crushed

Salt and freshly ground black pepper

Pinch of freshly grated nutmeg

2 cups Gruyère cheese grated on the large holes of a box grater

⅓ pound Smoked Scallops (about 15)

2 tablespoons minced fresh chives or fresh flat-leaf parsley

SERVES 4 AS A SIDE DISH

Preheat the oven to 375°F.

Bring the cream to a simmer in a large pot. Add the potatoes and simmer for 3 minutes.

Rub a 10-inch round baking dish with garlic. Leave the bits of torn garlic in the bottom of the dish.

Pour the potatoes and cream into the baking dish. Add salt and pepper to taste and the nutmeg and Gruyère. Bake, uncovered, for 20 minutes.

Remove the dish and gently fold in the scallops. Return the baking dish to the oven and continue cooking for about 15 minutes, until the top is golden. Garnish with fresh chives and serve.

ACKNOWLEDGMENTS

In preparing this book I talked to many home canners whose ideas and insights were invaluable, but special thanks go to my muses: Katherine McCarthy, Linda Rubick, Marilee Gilman, Elissa Rubin-Mahon, and Linda Long. I am grateful for the insights I received from Elizabeth L. Andress, PhD, of the National Center for Home Food Preservation. The Colorado State University Extension was super-helpful, especially Rhonda Follman of Mesa County and Karen Massey of Routt County, whose shoulders only drooped a tiny bit when I raised my hand for the billionth time during our Master Canner class. I benefitted greatly from many other extension offices operating out of state universities throughout the country, particularly Michigan State University Extension. I also learned a lot from the Seafood Network Information Center, the Fisheries Board of Canada, and the Agricultural Research Service at the Department of Agriculture. For their great kindness in reviewing the text on preservation techniques, many thanks to Marisa Bunning, PhD, and Mary Schroeder, MS, RD, of the Colorado State University Extension.

I owe a great debt of thanks to Megan Schlow and Andrew Brucker, both of whose work is interspersed throughout the book. Besides being talented photographers, they were my benevolent hand-holders as I muddled through this first color photography experience.

Thank you, Natalie Smith, proprietor of Global Table, the much copied and coolest tableware store in lower Manhattan. Natalie and I graduated from Barnard together— well, actually I don't think Natalie graduated. She's missing a fencing credit or something. Anyway, I must not have pissed her off too much at school, because years later we're still friends and she lent me all the props for the photos.

Thanks to my agent, Elise Goodman, whose apprehension about the whole canning thing pushed me to think very clearly, and Arnold Goodman—every writer needs a white knight. I really adored my original editor, Pam Krauss, who has since departed Clarkson Potter, and then guess what? It turned out my final editor, Judy Pray, was excellent in every way. In general, the team at Clarkson Potter—art director Jane Treuhaft and designer Amy Sly, Doris Cooper, Kate Tyler, Ava Kavyani, Donna Passanante, and Christine Tanigawa—all exhibited professionalism, enthusiasm, and were a pleasure to work with.

And finally, thanks to my family, Kevin, Carson, and Mo. They ate a lot of weird stuff in the process of my making this book, and they only complained a little.

INDEX